THE UNIVERSITY OF
WINCHESTER

Midday with Buñuel

Midday with Buñuel

MEMORIES AND SKETCHES, 1973–1983

Claudio Isaac

Translated by Bryan T. Scoular
With a Foreword by James D. Fernández

SWAN ISLE PRESS   CHICAGO

CLAUDIO ISAAC is a filmmaker, painter, novelist, poet, and contributor to various cultural journals and television arts programming in Mexico. Among his most recent films are *Eraclio Zepeda: Una mañana de mayo* and *Vlady: Pintar o morir*. He is also the author of *Alma húmeda*, a novel.

Swan Isle Press, Chicago 60640-8790
©2007 by Swan Isle Press
All rights reserved. Published 2007
Printed in the United States of America
11 10 09 08 07   1 2 3 4 5
ISBN-13: 978-0-9748881-3-2 (cloth)

www.swanislepress.com

Originally published in Mexico as : *Luis Buñuel: a mediodía*,co-edition © 2002 by CONACULTA (Consejo Nacional para la Cultura y las Artes); Universidad de Guadalajara; La Secretaria de Cultura de Colima; and reprinted in Spain by Fundación Centro Buñuel de Calanda, 2003. ©2001 by Claudio Isaac Rueda

Permissions granted by: The Isaac Family Archive; Lucero Isaac; Héctor J. Delgado, photograph of Luis Alcoriza de la Vega and Janet Riesenfeld Dunning de Alcoriza; "Photograph of Buñuel" © Man Ray Trust/Artists Rights Society (ARS) NY/ADAGP, Paris; Carlos Somonte, jacket photograph of Claudio Isaac; Javier Espada, director of Centro Buñuel de Calanda.

Swan Isle Press gratefully acknowledges that this book has been made possible, in part, with the support of generous grants from:

Program for Cultural Cooperation between Spain's Ministry of Culture and United States Universities

Swan Isle Press is funded in part by a generous grant from the Illinois Arts Council, A State of Illinois Agency

Europe Bay Giving Trust

Library of Congress Cataloging-in-Publication Data
Isaac, Claudio.
    [Luis Buñuel a mediodía. English]
    Midday with Buñuel : memories and sketches, 1973/1983 / Claudio Isaac ; translated by Bryan T. Scoular ; with a foreword by James D. Fernández. — 1st ed.
        p.   cm.
    Includes bibliographical references.
    ISBN 978-0-9748881-3-2
    1. Buñuel, Luis, 1900-1983—Anecdotes. 2. Motion picture producers and directors—Spain—Anecdotes. 3. Isaac, Claudio. I. Title.
    PN1998.3.B86183 2007
    791.4302'32092—dc22
    [B]   2007034187

For my wife, Valeria,

for Mauricio Maillé and for Pete Hamill,

thank you all for your insistence, for your generosity

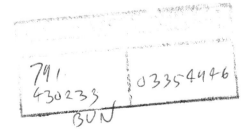

Contents

In the infinitude of time, the past and the future are interchangeable.

MAURICE MAETERLINCK, *The Life of Ants*

Foreword

Jorge Luis Borges once toyed with the idea of a biography
of Michelangelo that would avoid all references to the Ital-
ian master's works of art. Why not? It is only the tyranny of
teleology — the hindrances of hindsight — that obliges us
to reconstruct the artist's life as a garden path of works and
events leading inexorably toward the statue in the center:
the accomplished and consecrated figure of the "genius" we
all already know and love.

Once the biographer and his or her readers submit to the
rules of retrospective coherence, each biographical frag-
ment, each life episode — no matter how minor — seems
to become imbued with the force of foreshadow, invested
with the aura of inevitability. But we all know that life is so
much more complicated and hazardous than that. Why not,
Borges wonders, write a biography structured according to
the times that a subject has imagined the pyramids? Or according to the imperceptible but steady decline of a sub-

ject's bodily organs? Or according to the history of his or her " commerce with the night and with dawn"?

Of course, Claudio Isaac's *Midday with Buñuel* does not avoid all references to the vast filmography of his subject, one of the towering figures in the history of film. But those references are surprisingly — refreshingly — sparse. The reader in search of basic information regarding the more than thirty films made by Buñuel in the course of his varied and illustrious career would do much better elsewhere. As Isaac says in "Antecedents," this is "a book *with* Buñuel rather than a book *about* Buñuel." And in "Legacy," Isaac, himself a filmmaker, reveals that for him Buñuel was less "a mentor in cinema" than "a tutor for life."

Isaac, at the age of fifteen, had the privilege of being befriended by Buñuel — at the time in his seventies — and for the next ten years the two would regularly meet — often at noon sharp. This punctual and touching friendship is the focus of this literary scrapbook, in which Isaac sutures fragments of that lived experience, such as sketches, notes, and drafts from the period in question, together with retrospective musings from the writer's present moment: 2001.

Isaac is fully aware of some of the pitfalls common to such an approach. In one particularly admirable passage, he comments on his deeply ambivalent reaction to his own scraps of juvenilia, which, nonetheless, he dutifully transcribes in the book:

it is with a mix of dislike, compassion, affection, and laughter that I look upon this wise young man, dogmatic and pedantic […], plagued by […] worries about purity and goodness, honesty and transcendence, even in one of its least noble guises: personal fame. There are [in these transcribed fragments] as much levity as solemnity, there is shyness and insecurity right beside cockiness and petulance.

Significantly, these "confessions" are simultaneously "exhibitions," and the writer knows this. Things would be so much easier if we could just draw up a two-column ledger and list on one side those things we are proud of and, on the other, those that bring us shame or make us blush. But Isaac reminds us, alas, that pride and shame often dwell together. We are before a self-conscious and contradictory chronicle of contradictions.

And contradiction, it would seem, is also the distinctive feature of Luis Buñuel. Isaac's unflinching perception of these contradictions forestalls the elaboration of a solemn hagiography of an illustrious mentor. The Buñuel that emerges from this patchwork of fragments and memories is both timid and theatrical, enamored of spontaneity and bound to routine, freedom loving and, at the same time, authoritarian.

A "biography" of Luis Buñuel that is structured not by the stepping-stones of his career, but by the self-spun spider's web of his many contradictions, as they are perceived, assimilated, and recorded by a chronicler who is himself always in motion and full of contradictions. I think Borges might have approved of this approach to the genre. Borges claimed, after all, that his hypothetical biography of an artist that omitted references to his artwork could serve as a kind of blueprint for modern literature, a literature that explores "life itself, with all its minutiae and all its profound enigmas"(96). And, I would add, with all its admirable and shameful contradictions.

JAMES D. FERNÁNDEZ
Madrid, Residencia de Estudiantes
27 January, 2007

For Further Reading

FOR ENGLISH-SPEAKING READERS:

Buñuel. Luis. *My Last Sigh*. Translated by Abigail Israel. Minneapolis: University of Minnesota Press, 2003.

Buñuel, Luis. *An Unspeakable Betrayal: Selected Writings of Luis Buñuel*. Translated by Garrett White. Berkeley: University of California Press, 2000.

Edwards, Gwynne. *The Discreeet Art of Luis Buñuel: A Reading of His Films*. New York and London: Marion Boyars, 1982.

Evans, Peter William. *The Films of Buñuel: Subjectivity and Desire*. Oxford: Clarendon Press, 1995.

Evans, Peter William, and Isabel Santaolalla, eds. *Luis Buñuel: New Readings*. London: British Film Institute, 2004.

Sandro, Paul. *Diversions of Pleasure: Luis Buñuel and the Crises of Desire*. Columbus: Ohio State University Press, 1987.

FOR SPANISH-SPEAKING READERS:

Rucar de Buñuel, Jeanne. *Memorias de una mujer sin piano*. With Marisol Martin del Campo. Madrid: Alianza Editorial, 1991.

Sánchez Vidal, Agustin. *Luis Buñuel*. Madrid: Cátedra, 2004.

Sánchez, Agustin. *Lorca, Buñuel y Dalí: el enigma sin fin*. Madrid: Planeta, 1988.

Sánchez Vidal also collaborated on the excellent documentary by José Luis López Linares and Javier Rioyo, titled *A propósito de Buñuel*. Claudio Isaacs is interviewed in the film.

Translator's Note

In *Mi último suspiro* (*My Last Sigh*), Luis Buñuel, in a chapter titled "earthly delights," tells of how he would let his mind meander as his eyes followed the snaking branches of a tree. He writes that in front of the bar of San José Puruá Hotel, in Michoacán,

there was a ziranda — a tropical tree with curving branches interlaced like a nest of huge snakes[...]. My eyes would follow aimlessly along the myriad intersections of the branches; sometimes I'd put an owl on one of them, or a naked woman, or some other incongruous element.
[TRANSLATED BY ABIGAIL ISRAEL, P. 43]

It is tempting to use this tree as a metaphor for many of Luis Buñuel's most important films: from *Un Chien andalou* and *L'Âge d'or* to *La Charme discrète de la bourgeoise* and *Le Fantôme de la liberté*, they consist of series of disparate scenes full of incongruous elements that are woven together in such an expert way that they become transformed into works of art that are both cohesive and compelling. As they say in Spanish, the films *se van por las ramas*, or go off on tangents, but nevertheless achieve a sense of wholeness.

The *ziranda* might also be seen as a fitting metaphor for Claudio Isaac's *Midday with Buñuel*, which is written not as a conventional, linear biography nor memoir, but as a series of short narrative fragments that, together, form an organic and intricate image of the legendary filmmaker in his later years and self-portrait of an artist as a young man in the context of their friendship and their lives in Mexico. The fragmentary nature of the memoir is, to my mind, one of the work's main strengths, as it underlines the self-reflexive, or overtly subjective, stance of the author in its very form. Especially challenging was to replicate in tone the many sentence fragments, which function as a mirror to the fragmentary and terse nature of text that frames them.

Many of Claudio Isaac's remembrances of Buñuel are narrated as conversations, and where there is not explicit dialogue, the text still conserves an element of orality. This is achieved largely through a lack of conjunctions and an insistence on the present tense when speaking of past events, which gives the impression of a story being told with immediacy and presence, punctuated by lively, idiomatic observations. I have tried as far as possible to retain this stylistic quality and general rhythm of the Spanish text. In other words, I hope my translation has been, to use a favorite word of Buñuel's, discreet.

BRYAN T. SCOULAR
Geneva, Switzerland
February 2007

Acknowledgments

About eight or nine years ago, when I finally decided to organize the notes about Luis Buñuel that I had accumulated and turn them into a book, I informed his sons Rafael and Juan Luis of my intentions in a letter. I felt it was my obligation to let them know about my plans from the outset, though I foresaw that their reaction would be between reluctant, self-conscious, and uncomfortable. First, I knew they were against any kind of tribute because they respected their father's ideas about dignity, which included a rejection of sentimentalities. Also, though they loved their father, his enormous figure cast a long shadow over their families' lives, and they were worn out from the countless acts of homage that had recently been celebrated on the occasion of Buñuel's centenary. Their answers to my letter were vague, almost apathetic despite the cordial friendship that we had enjoyed for years, but they gave a cryptic and lukewarm approval. Soon after, Juan Luis wrote a letter to my mother that in essence amounted to a tacit validation: "I have learned about the book that Claudio is planning to write about my father. Ay, it is one *more* book about the topic. But, in the end, they loved each other so much that the book must be of value."

After the publication of *Luis Buñuel: a mediodía*, the idea inevitably surfaced that I might have wished to show off as an expert or authority on the man and his work. Nothing could be further from the truth. As I have declared elsewhere, for a long time I tried to keep my notebooks to myself and leave Buñuel deservedly in peace. But the book project imposed itself on me: It arises from a pleasant debt of pure affection.

I would like to let the reader know that there were two previous editions of this book in Spanish. In 2002, the generous editor Cristina Martín recommended that my text be published by the University of Guadalajara, Mexico. Thanks to them and with additional support from the Ministry of Culture of the State of Colima and the National Council for Culture and the Arts (CONACULTA), *Luis Buñuel: a mediodía* appeared for the first time. The next year, the actor Arturo Beristáin proposed to the cultural attaché to the Mexican Embassy in Spain, the poet Alejandro Aura, that a copy of the recently published book be sent to Javier Espada, the dynamic director of the Buñuel Center in Calanda (CBC), a stupendous little museum, paradoxically situated in an abandoned small town in which the tumbleweeds, blown by the wind from the *páramo*, roll around in the main square. Although I was warmly received by all of the locals, who were all memorable people, I felt as if I had entered into the spectral landscape of one of Juan Rulfo's novels: walled-up windows, worn-down doors with rusty locks, streets without people. Espada, who founded a functional avant-garde space while conserving the rudimentary nature of the locale in which Buñuel was born in 1900, welcomed the project and enthusiastically published a second edition. Both the Conaculta and Calanda editions in the original language were brought to light by admirable editorial efforts, for which I will always be thankful. I am now grateful to Swan Isle Press for publishing this first English-language edition.

I would also like to express my appreciation to James Fernández for his contribution to this project on many levels, including his foreword to this edition. Finally, regarding this first edition in English, so faithfully translated by Bryan Scoular, I would like to affirm that I am pleased that the scenes I narrate retain the spirit of the original Spanish. This, for me, counterbalances the nagging temptation, years later, of rewriting.

CLAUDIO ISAAC
Mexico City
January 2007

Midday with Buñuel

Drawing from 1977

Prologue

Due to its nature, this book is partial in its opinions and fragmentary in form. Just like the truth game, it is nourished by omissions.

Luis Buñuel was a man who had an almost sacred sense of privacy. While in these notes I pry into some of the most intimate interstices of his life, I have sincerely tried not to betray his modesty.

I met him during my childhood, with my parents. But it was not until my first years of adolescence, when I was certain that I would dedicate myself to filmmaking, that I tried to make his acquaintance.

Overcoming some unfavorable conditions — to begin with, he couldn't stand children, and I still looked like a boy — I was able to gain entrance, alone, into his house.

Some kind of spark of affinity or sympathy must have marked our first encounter: a week later I visited him again. During many more meetings, we would develop a relationship which, due to generational differences, was constrained by countless reserves, prejudices, and incompatibilities but, given that it was grounded in affection, grew into a profound friendship. I am sure that Luis would say the same.

From this friendship over ten years between a wise, rebellious old man of eighty and an awkward novice of fifteen come the following pages.

The First Thing

Upon invoking him, the first thing that comes into focus is the radiance in the greenness of those brusquely asymmetrical eyes. I remember you, Luis Buñuel. Vividly.

Luis, ca. 1973

The Entomologist

Some years after the death of Buñuel, a television program reunited various actors who had worked with him in Mexico. They were to give their opinion about Luis as a director. In the struggle to stand out from the rest with a memorable anecdote, all of them tended to extol him and attribute virtues to him that were never his.

"I was never clear about the dialogues, but the *maestro* went over them with me patiently and in detail until everything came out right…"

"I had never received so much attention as an actress until I worked with Luis. That gentleman understood us perfectly…"

The distorted and solemn subject matter of the program inevitably reminded me of a dialogue I had with Luis at the beginning of 1980.

"Luis," I said to him, "I am reading the book that Truffaut wrote about Alfred Hitchcock."

"I haven't read it," he responded. "Is it good?"

"It's a lot of fun. He tells an anecdote about when Hitchcock made a movie with Carole Lombard. At some distance, she overheard him say that actors were cattle. The very next day, Lombard had a cowshed made on the set where they were filming. And when Hitchcock arrived to work he found the actors of the film behind a fence, mooing."

With a jovial expression, Luis reflected in silence for a few moments. He frowned and declared in a stern, exalted voice: "What do you mean, cattle?...Cockroaches, worse than cockroaches. I roll up newspapers and squash them on the walls..."

Thus spake Buñuel the entomologist.

Luis, ca. 1969

A Day in the Countryside

The first impression was surely severe: the pronounced cheekbones, the rough nose of the pugilist, the harsh jawbone that was finished off by a square chin, and his mouth, with tense lips, that arched downwards. While beneath the surface there might have been fragility or tenderness, my child's sensibility led me to read something perturbing in his expression, to both the disparity of the eyelids and the resounding weight of his gaze.

I must have been six years old, and we were in the countryside. That's what the photographs that survive indicate. I suppose it was midday on a Sunday and I was one of only three or four kids who were dying of boredom in a huge, dry cornfield. None of us knew each other, and we were separated from the animated conversation of the adults — my parents and the other married couple, who were enjoying the *sobremesa*, or after-meal chat, in the terrace adjacent to the simple little structure with a two-gutter roof that formed a cabin of sorts.

My truncated reminiscences about that time we all shared together in the countryside are woven together from those few photographic images and with the versions that, over the years, the others who were there have added to the memory of the group. As a result, the first recollections I have of Buñuel are frayed and tenuous, like the memory of a memory.

I invent for myself this plausible scenario: My natural attraction for older people leads me away from the playmates imposed by children's games, and I approach some bushes

A day in the countryside: Luis Buñuel, Claudio Isaac, and Isaac's mother, Lucero, ca. 1961

that, despite their scanty foliage, make me feel sheltered. I can closely observe that scene in which everyone seemed to be having a good time. Buñuel always participates in the conversation, but once in a while, as if responding to his aversion to the presence of children, he would look over to the area of the cornfield with a scrutinizing stare. Despite his poor eyesight, he immediately detects my presence behind the precarious branches that I have chosen as a refuge. Without making any gesture, he obliges me to return to where the other kids are. The half-distance allows me to pretend

The cabin of my childhood memories

that I haven't seen anything, and that no one has seen me. But I obey. I must have walked on tiptoe in a cautious and ridiculous retreat. All of this I imagine in precise detail.

Of course, neither at six nor at nine years of age was I exactly aware of the role my parents' friend played on the world's stage. I liked his soft, hoarse voice, the shine of his dark skin, his forehead and its crisscrossed wrinkles, and the scant, fine, ash-colored hair that adorned his head, which had been stained by the sun and the passing of time. I also was intrigued by his exaggerated gestures and the way he dramatically waved his arms as he spoke. He seemed to me a strangely magnetic person indeed. But, in the end, he was first and foremost an old man — even older than my grandfather, the oldest person I knew.

A Banquet

One time Luis told me an anecdote from the fifties: during a banquet in the Churubusco Studios he was seated next to someone he did not know. The waiters served them wine. Upon trying it, Luis said: It tastes awful.

Indignant, the man beside him announced: For your information, I produce it.

The moment was embarrassing, but without much hesitation, Luis responded: Well, I give you permission to speak badly of my films.

Emilio García Riera, Luis Buñul, and Alberto Isaac, ca. 1964

Jeanne

Of a beautifully infantile spirit, Jeanne was goodness incarnate, the absence of malevolence. Each day she renewed her repertory of innocent jokes, prepared tricks, or "practical jokes"; a fake bloody finger, a rag doll that gave out a sinister laugh, even a mask with glasses, false nose, and mustache that she put on once in a while to open the front door. There were also, in different sizes, rubber spiders. A strange morbidity, declared Luis's sister Conchita, makes spiders the principal subject of family conversations.

She liked people to call her Juana or Juanita. Jeanne was a large woman: tall and strong. Playful but did not smile very much. One of her most disconcerting gestures was to freeze her face in a very pronounced smile, deliberately false. For all the visitors to the house she did tricks with a lit cigarette, confessed to them her weakness for marrons glacés, showed them her Olympic medal, and opened her heart to them, truly. She never lied, she didn't know how to.

Luis

Luis, on the contrary, detested set jokes, the prefabricated character of rakish stories. For him, humor was synonymous with spontaneity; it flowed from an unforeseen situation, from the current of the conversation. He liked to develop jokes on the spur of the moment, to stage them. For this he required accomplices.

"We're all going to act offended by Colina. When he enters, no one is to speak to him or look at him."

Usually these jokes flopped prematurely because somebody would break out laughing, wrecking the drama. No one could keep up with Luis, who had an amazing capability of staying serious, of prolonging a rigidity of expression until he managed to make the atmosphere frankly unbreathable.

Luis and Jeanne, ca. 1969

The Bar

Entering the house through the front door, one saw a small room to the right, which served the functions of sitting room and cantina. Rarely was the living room used.

Given that they drank in that room, it was called the bar. Regulated by the drapes, the light always seemed the same. Around a low table with doilies and ash trays, a large armchair against the wall and two chairs of heavy wood of an ersatz colonial Mexican style. Adorning them were colorful cushions Jeanne had embroidered after designs that the sculptor Alexander Calder had sent her.

In a corner a refrigerator—not a portable apparatus of medium height, but a huge white piece of furniture that hummed a little. In it there were only olives and ice. Occasionally serrano ham. On the wall behind it hung an enormous map of the Paris subway. On one of the other walls, a long shelf with the basic utensils of a barman: ice buckets, cocktail shakers, cocktail stirrers, bottle openers. They shared the space with some of Jeanne's offspring: her dolls and gadgets, some of the objects for her jokes—above all, the newest ones were placed there for show.

On the ledge, more glasses and bottles of all types. In the center, a wooden frame that held, successively, engravings of Gironella or Julián Pablo Fernández, or my drawings in ink. People understood that they were grateful for gifts of that kind, and they exhibited them. I would dare say they were indifferent to the content of the works. (Take, for example, Dalí's portrait of Luis, its presence on a square column at the entrance to the living room, which he always apologized for, saying it was there only for nostalgic reasons.) Also, a false identity card of a gendarme with a three-cornered hat and a five o'clock shadow had come to rest above the ledge without requiring explanation. It was Colonel Tejero, that frustrated coup leader, who took the Spanish congress in the eighties.

We could add the presence of Tristana, the mouse-hunting terrier (*perra ratonera andaluza*). Sitting on the armchair, she was a witness to illimitable sessions of cigarette smoke, drinking, and conversations.

Tristana

Luis and my Father

Although they met each other at the end of the fifties, when one looks back one finds that the rapprochement between Buñuel and my father began in 1962, when *Viridiana*, recently filmed in Francoist Spain, was shown at the Cannes Film Festival. On the occasion of that screening, my father published a cartoon in praise of Buñuel, who had been prejudged and condemned by a great part of the community of Spanish exiles and the intellectual community in Mexico, who considered the filmmaker a traitor who had embraced Franco's regime. The drawing generated interest well beyond Mexico City, and it was published in international magazines and even in monographs, thereby becoming a kind of emblem for Buñuel's cause. Buñuel never forgot favors, and it seems likely that my father's gesture sealed their friendship.

In 1965, when my father directed his first film, *En este pueblo no hay ladrones* (*There Are No Thieves in This Village*) he invited Luis to interpret the role of a bitter and intimidating traditional priest. The commission was not merely a wink to the alert spectator, however, as the character had a fair bit of dialogue, which Luis had to memorize.

Due to that unexpected appearance, generations of scholars continue to go over the movie year after year.

Alberto Isaac: VINI, VIDI, VINCI

15

When Luis was face to face with my father, he called him Alberto, but when he referred to him he called him by his last name, Isaac, stretching out the double "a" as if it were an interminable tunnel.

For his part, my father was attentive with Luis. He liked to indulge him, once in a while giving him rare liquors or books, taking him out to his favorite restaurants.

I should mention that my father understood from the start that he was in the presence of a living legend, but his healthy indifference to the splendors of immortality kept the relationship very down to earth.

I close my eyes and I see them together: Luis and my father had a relationship of mutual respect and, moreover, of true warmth. But above all they laughed. They always laughed. I would dare say that their affection was manifested most of all in their shared laughter.

Luis Buñuel and Alberto Isaac, ca. 1969

Luis and My Mother

One afternoon when my mother got home she told me that at the department store two blocks down from the Buñuels' house (not to be confused with the gigantic hardware shop one block away) she had seen Luis, looking like a lost kid, intently studying the buttons in a store window. She then took him shopping against his will—despite his pleading, complaining, and general bashfulness. My mother, who never had much money but who, if I remember correctly,

Buñuel and Lucero Isaac on a street of the Churubusco Studios, ca. 1973

had recently gotten paid for a job, bought him a two-piece summer suit and had made Luis, who was virtually kicking and screaming, try it on in the dressing room. Later, when they were leaving the store, my mother put a gob of sample lotion in the hollow of her hands and rubbed it into Luis's face. Taking hold of him by the shoulders, she then gave him a light shove toward the exit.

"Now go home," she ordered him, "and tell Jeanne that you just went for a short walk."

Although this story might sound unbelievable, it is in fact quite typical of my mother and Luis Buñuel. She loved him and loved to tease him; it aroused in her an adolescent enthusiasm for making mischief. In response to these games, Luis feigned impatience but deep down in his watery eyes one could see that he enjoyed the provocations. And that he was moved. Well, the anecdote passed to the home archive of the improbable, a collection pregnant with stories of adventures with priests, whose churches she divested of precious objects, of cops running after her on their motorbikes, and of publicly insulting women working for charities. One day Luis appeared for dinner in his new suit of "thousand-stripes" cloth, and, blushing again, with his eyes wide open and a hand in the air, he told his animated version of the story:

"None of you know what Lucerito has put me through…"

"And the shock on the faces of the store clerks!"

I saw that fragile expression on Luis Buñuel's face time and again. Even in his most intricate machinations there was always a touch of candor.

The Two Luises

The nights that there were get-togethers at our house, I would spy on the guests from the nave of the staircase. In a dark corner, wearing a flannel nightshirt, I furtively watched Luis Buñuel countless times. Secreted in the mezzanine, I was a witness to the conduct of the adults in the small, well-lighted living room, full of cigarette smoke and sounds: the tinkling of glasses filled with whisky and the continuous laughs and shouts.

One time, Luis Buñuel and Luis Alcoriza were going at it for a long time after dinner.

"You're frivolous," Buñuel said.

"You're monkish," replied Alcoriza.

"You're conceited..."

"You're a bore..."

They continued this way for a while, until they got to the issue of clothes, of the other's choice of attire.

"You have your pants cut like a pimp's," Buñuel declared.

"And you wear them so loose that the rise is down to your knees," Alcoriza answered him.

By some arbitrary turn of their argument, Buñuel and Aloriza ended up exchanging trousers. They traded them in the hallway adjacent to the living room, and then returned to show the rest of the group. The laughs were louder than ever at the sight of the foppish Alcoriza in baggy trousers that went up to his ribcage and Buñuel, showcasing his virility, in a pair as close-fitting as the tights of a ballet dancer or circus performer.

Luis Buñuel, Alberto Isaac, and Luis Alcoriza, ca. 1964

Husbands and Wives

Another completely innocent joke that my parents and the Buñuels constantly played at social get-togethers was to tell the others present that Luis was my mother's husband and that Jeanne my father's wife. Jeanne would kiss my father on the cheek continuously and noisily, while my mother would sit down on Luis's lap. The joke did not go any further. That story spawned another, in which I was Jeanne's third son.

Lucero Isaac and Luis Buñuel, ca. 1975

Sulphates

In those years of my childhood, I had no contact at all with Luis. Caring and sympathy came exclusively from Jeanne, who was always generous with the affection she gave me. "Where is my son?" she would say in her candid way of playing, asking for me as soon as she arrived for a visit at our house.

Now, when she visits me in my dreams, I always try to remember the prescription of sulphates with which she cured me of a cold when I was nine or ten years old.

Claudio and Jeanne, ca. 1971

Competition

When adolescence arrived, and with it a more precise idea of the value of the cinema (to which, as I have mentioned already, I would soon dedicate myself), I plucked up the courage to approach Buñuel. As a young, self-taught filmmaker, in equal measures impetuous and unsure, it seemed crucial to me to confront him so that he would recognize me as an individual. But it wasn't such an easy undertaking. I began to go out with my father to meetings and parties with people from the movies, and always felt at ease. Although nobody was nearly as young, a benevolent heterogeneity prevailed.

Even though I still looked like a boy, Luis Buñuel didn't mind my presence anymore. On the other hand, he was worried that people would say dirty words when I was around. Due to a tutelary idiosyncrasy, he felt inhibited and uncomfortable: how was he going to let loose a "cunt" (*coño*) in front of the boy?

I should say that whenever I saw Luis in public, it was the end of a propitious social climate for me. The relaxed atmosphere of familiarity that existed between the Buñuels, the Alcorizas, and my parents disappeared. In the circles formed by critics, filmmakers, and intellectuals of Mexico City, it was difficult to breathe easily in the presence of Buñuel, as they all crowded around him, immersed in childish competition and pressed by the tyrannical constraints of time. It was not an assumed matter but, of course, there existed a servile contest to get Luis's attention, with notorious exceptions. I can't prove that I am making an objective description. These were the people who obstructed my path to Luis, cut me off when I began to speak, and jealously tried to eclipse me.

I tried to participate in the conversations time and again, but I wasn't able to get in a phrase edgeways. But after a while, some months later, I find the way to free myself from them and avoid that abusive and ridiculous rivalry.

Carlos Savage, Luis Buñuel, Alberto Isaac, Luis Alcoriza, Luis González de León, and Emilio García Riera (reclining on table)

Two Letters

I already mentioned that when I gave him one of my drawings as a gift, he would display it on one of the shelves in the main part of the bar. That was his way of thanking me; the gesture was never accompanied by any opinion whatsoever. He esteemed and respected me, but that did not mean he was overly approving or enthusiastic of what I could do. As the reader already gathers, he was very consistent with his feelings.

In 1981, when I was organizing the production of my second feature-length film, *El día que murió Pedro Infante (The Day Pedro Infante Died)*, Luis offered to support my effort. We planned two letters together. The first, directed to Gustavo Alatriste, producer of his last films in Mexico, asking him to see me and read my screenplay. We tried in vain to enlist his help in financing the project.

The second letter he directed to me. Clearly, as we lived in the same city and saw each other regularly, it was implicit that this letter was written so that I could use it, so I could take advantage of the weight his name carried to open doors. But it didn't help either.

Even so, I remember how much fun it was to work out our strategy. He wrote the letter in private, but we had previously discussed the details.

"I can't praise you too much," he said. "In order for it to be credible, I'm going to say that I don't like the title and that you should find a better one…"

Carta a Gustavo Alatriste

México 18 Novbre 81

Querido Gustavo:

Con la presente irá a visi
tarte Claudio Isaac, hijo de nues
tro común amigo Alberto. Un
mozo muy inteligente y buen ci-
neasta, que quiere hablar contigo
sobre un asunto que le interesa.
Mucho te agradeceré que lo re
cibas.

Un abrazo,

Luis Buñuel

P. S. — Leí el guión de Claudio
y creo en sus posibilidades
llevado a la pantalla.

Letter from Buñuel to producer Gustavo Alatriste, 1981

It also occurred to him—and this was the most generous concession he made for me—to mention in passing Margarita López Portillo, the sister of the president in power and head of the state cinema at that time. "If you take it to doña Margarita it's a done deal," said the letter, or something like that. But this lady did not react at all to the letter when I showed it to her.

carta a Claudio Isaac

Mexico 6 Julio 71

Querido Claudio: He leido su script y me ha gustado. Creo en tu talento y con esa base puedes hacer un buen film. Lo unico que no me agrada es el titulo. Pero eso puede cambiarse y encontrar otro mejor. Te sugiero que se lo lleves a Doña Margarita y si a ella le interesa, es cosa hecha, quiero decir, film realizado. Dame no- ticias de como marcha su asunto.

Un abrazo de

Luis Buñuel

Letter from Buñuel to Claudio Isaac, 1981 (The date on the letter is an error.)

None of You Understand

Margarita was the natural villain for several generations of filmmakers accustomed to the protection of the State, a patronage that was started under Rodolfo Echeverría, the brother of the former president of the republic and director of the Cinematographic Bank. People always made cruel jokes and bitter commentaries — all well deserved — about Margarita, whom they gave the moniker Macartita for her witch hunts in the style of Joe McCarthy. They also called her the pitiful (*pésima*) muse for her obsession with imitating sor Juana Inés de la Cruz, who was called the tenth (*décima*) muse in all of the official school textbooks. Although I was a victim of her attacks more than once, I never bore her a grudge: because of her very fine white skin and her sparkling eyes, she reminded me too much of my aunt Mini, a prodigy of sweetness and charity. And, of course, if my aunt Mini had been in charge of the country's media, she would have also caused havoc and disaster, accustomed as she was to knitting and taking tea with her friends in the peace of her living room. But I should return to Luis. Despite the fact that he was of the same mind with those who attacked Margarita and made fun of her, he always had a strange weakness for this corpulent woman of fine features.

"None of you understand," he explained to us. "Margarita is a sensual woman."

The matter always drew ridicule and, as I remember, these were the only occasions when, among the circle of filmmakers in Mexico, there was an open and generalized irreverence toward Luis. On the other hand, a fresh and invigorating event.

The Son of a Civil Servant

After the crest of the political capriciousness embodied by Margarita surged a wave of antinepotism. Ironically, in the next government my father was named director of the Institute of Cinematography, and, as a result, I found a new obstacle in my career in the cinema: the son of the civil servant cannot work here. Out of the frustration that I experienced at this time, I sometimes called my father "Don Margarito."

Alberto Isaac in the costume that Buñuel would later wear, in his first film, En este pueblo no hay ladrones *(There Are No Thieves in This Village)*

Reading My Screenplay

After reading my screenplay for *El día que murió Pedro Infante* (*The Day Pedro Infante Died*), Luis made a few specific commentaries. One of them was the following: toward the climax of the film there was a long dialogue between an editor and a young novelist. In it I had poured all of the ideological charge that I felt was indispensable, given that these were the peak years of political cinema. On this Luis was categorical: This scene, bad. Cut all of the dialogue, all nine pages, no explanations. The novelist enters, the editor tells him, "We don't like your book." The novelist exits.

I didn't heed his advice but I am convinced he was absolutely right.

Tears

In September 1982, probably after having seen *Un chien andalou (An Andalousian Dog)* again, I wrote a text, a kind of short poem in prose. As I knew that reading was becoming difficult for him and that he sometimes had to use a magnifying glass on a stand to look over some documents, I transcribed the words with a thick marker on a big sheet of paper.

I took it to him without being able to conquer my nerves. I knew I was getting myself into doubly delicate terrain, and I was afraid first that Luis would get upset if he saw me as pretentious in my literary effort; even worse, the intention of rendering him homage was inscribed in sentimental territory, which he usually did not tolerate or allow at all.

I arrived at his house, and the first thing I did was give him the page that was written with the black marker.

"Hey, what's this?" he asked with genuine surprise. Although he had the magnifying glass just a few steps away, he preferred not to use it. In fact, he took off his glasses and, stretching out his arm, held out the sheet of paper at a distance. Proud of being able to decipher the text without his glasses, he read it in its entirety aloud without pausing. Upon concluding, he sighed deeply and told me, "Kid, I love you a lot."

He didn't allow his eyes to tear up completely, and in order to free himself from an emotional moment (as if avoiding passing a literary judgment), he escaped by way of a humorous tangent: "O.K. I am going to issue a formal decree that everyone should use this brand of thick pen to write to Luis Buñuel."

My tears (I had experienced an immediate mimetic reaction) turned into tears of laughter, of laughter and of relief: I had gone out on a limb, and everything turned out great.

Luis Buñuel in the pulpit in the film En este pueblo no hay ladrones (There Are No Thieves in This Village)

Poem

The text, as it was published (in Spanish), years later, in a newspaper:

Once I had the idea that to Magritte will always belong the moment when night falls and the silhouettes of the trees appear as cutouts, markedly dark, against a profound and luminous sky.

Tonight the clouds have been crossing in front of the moon—time and again, in elongated formations. Inevitably I have thought of eyes and razor blades and I have confirmed that after 1928 this occasional image of the cosmos belongs to you, Luis Buñuel.

Cardinal Virtue

"Not a minute before, and not a minute after: that is punctuality," said Luis, who was always annoyed with the tardiness, the inexactitude, of Mexicans.

"A lack of respect for others," he used to grumble, and I, a precocious stickler for punctuality, agreed.

Without his having to tell me, I preferred to arrive a little early and window shop on the avenue close to the Buñuels' house, or drop into a stationery store and look around before going to the Cerrada de Félix Cuevas and walk the last inexorable steps, my heart beating fast, nervous about meeting Luis Buñuel.

After two months of visiting him, I knew the sequence of façades of the neighbors' houses, the dogs on the block, and I greeted some of the neighbors as if they were old friends.

I knew, from waiting the last minutes and seconds for the appointed hour, the cracks in the sidewalk in front of his house.

When the clock struck noon, I approached the large, gray metal door and rang the bell no more than once.

From one of Buñuel's autobiographical statements published years later I discovered the origin of his obsession with punctuality. It seems to have arisen out of some unfortunate amorous episodes from his early youth: mortifying, torturous waits, dates at fixed hours that would make his heart race.

When I began to visit him, he liked my impeccable punctuality and congratulated me for it as if it were a cardinal virtue. He didn't know that, being the adolescent I was, I already suffered from love stories similar to his, dates in which the ticking of the clock was for me, as it had been for him, a source of torment. The curious thing is that though we differed in age by fifty-seven years, a common neurotic trait could unite us, neither a minute too early nor a minute too late.

Claudio and Luis under a fig tree

Hearing and Not Hearing

To figure out where her deaf husband was in the house, Jeanne would make an extremely sharp noise not unlike that of a dog whistle or a screaming teakettle. When guests were over, this embarrassed him, and it bothered him that she did it. She knew this and tried not to mortify him in front of company, but sometimes she did it without meaning to, from force of habit.

He would come rushing down the stairs, exclaiming, "But I'm not deaf, woman."

As a counterpart to this recurring episode, there were occasions when Luis feigned deafness in order to avoid some domestic chores.

"Luis," Jeanne would say, appearing with the terrier on a leash, "it's your turn to take Tristana for a walk…"

"What?…" Luis would answer, putting his hand behind his ear, representing the stereotypical image of a deaf man. "Mrs. Santa Anna wants to talk?"

The dialogue would continue a little longer. Luis pretended to not understand a word; Jeanne would roll her eyes, turn around, and disappear with the dog. As soon as she had departed, he would lodge his complaint with me:

"As if I'm going to walk the dog…She has to be kidding."

Lip Reading

In social settings Luis Buñuel was, above all, reserved and laconic. In public he gave the impression of accentuating his introspectiveness. I recall in particular an intense, clear image: his incredibly profound, faraway look, which betrayed his detachment from the world. I discovered him in that trance many times, in the middle of a banquet room, among the agitation of crossing conversations. Suspended in a meditative quietness, like a monk in prayer, surrounded by the feverish hustle of a marketplace.

He could also become a mordant misanthrope: observing him out of the corner of my eye or at a distance, I learned how to decipher his gestures that indicated, for example, that when faced with the long-winded chatter of an insatiable interlocutor, he had decided to turn off his hearing aid. With a slight smile, he would look dispassionately at the speaker, hearing now only a murmur. I suppose that the impishness of his private joke kept alive that smile, which others interpreted as a friendly sign of condescension.

On the other hand, I can remember many times when, especially in a noisy room, in order to follow a conversation that clearly interested him, he would have to concentrate on the speaker's lips and try to read them.

Vignette

In 1972, when I had recently started to make eight-millimeter films (which were an important part of my autodidactic formation), Luis proposed an idea to me. It consisted, as in all of these cinematic exercises, which were only six or seven minutes long, of what amounted to an uncomplicated vignette to be interpreted by my friend, the actor Arturo Beristáin.

"A guy ties a tie continuously," explained Luis, illustrating his idea with expressions and gestures. "Then he straightens the lapels of his jacket, he brushes his mustache , all in an orderly and methodical fashion. He has an immaculate desk: the papers are stacked in the center and the letter opener is parallel to the pens. At lunchtime he leaves his office and begins to feel uncomfortable; he has a foreboding of something. In a cold sweat, visibly nervous, he returns to the office and sees that he has left a desk drawer open. He closes it and sighs in relief. The End."

The extremely simple subject was perfect for the kind of basic narrative challenges for which I was searching for my improvement as a filmmaker. Strangely, it corresponded both to my personal eccentricities as a precocious fifteen-year-old (which I have already mentioned) and to a clearly Buñuelesque spirit. In his generous manner, Luis had the gift of suggesting solutions that were not only viable but also very characteristic of him.

Something about Me

To begin with, Luis never approved of my parents' divorce. He never really understood why the divorce was not a traumatic event for me or why I might have chosen to live with my father. In those matters his recondite Puritanism surfaced. As a result of our solitary lives, at the height of my adolescence, I developed with my father a lively relationship between bachelors with a full social life of dinners, parties, trips — above all trips related to the cinema: festivals and filmings.

But everything was not carousing and partying. I also carried on a parallel life of solemn sorrows and the torments of unconfessed loves. I attributed transcendence to everything that happened to me, and so I made myself miserable.

I will give an example of this to situate myself, as a character, in the years that most of these pages cover. Unconfessable loves, I was saying. The most profound and desperate of all was my love for the actress Helena Rojo. I had met her at the gigantic birthday party of a splendid figure from the artistic crowd: Irma Serrano, a singer and star of Mexican westerns, or *rancheras*, who had a reputation as a man-eater because of her tumultuous love affair with President Díaz Ordaz. It was winter, and the hostess had some of her countrymen (from Chiapas) playing the marimba by the pool. The poor musicians wore wool hats and scarves and exhaled vapor while they played. Inside, behind the large windows, we were warmed by a sizable open fire.

Helena must be almost ten years older than I. She literally dazzled me. When she emerged from the shadows of an arc and approached a thundering fountain of light, she was, for me, the incarnation of melancholic beauty. Consequently, as a youth with Wertherian airs, I became doubly infatuated: with a love of beauty and with an inclination to melancholy.

As one might expect, time went by, and I could not erase her face from my mind. I developed all the symptoms of stupor, ceaseless and sterile speculation, and the disquiet of platonic love. Love for imbeciles.

The furthest I got was to cook up a way for her to collaborate with me in the filmic trials I was carrying out. Indeed, Helena Rojo acted in more than ten of those films, which were so brief and insignificant in appearance, yet so essential for me, so intimate. I took pleasure in directing her, filming her. But I was incapable of telling her anything about what was burning me up inside. Moreover, when she showed up late for a call, my suffering was redoubled: as a budding cineaste with professional aspirations and as a lover, albeit a tragicomical one. In a decision that came out of my crazy possessiveness (which seems to me today at the same time moving, curious, and ridiculous), I decided to film Helena's scenes alone with her even if they included dialogue between various characters. My stylistic preference for fragmenting the scenes into closed frames and fixed shots worked well with this idea: I worked with the various actors—Beristáin, Diana Bracho, or Alfonso Arau—separately, but after editing it seemed as if they had been filmed together.

Of course, my desire was logged in my journal of unreciprocated love. (How on earth was it going to be any other way—reciprocated—if my first confession of it is this public declaration almost thirty years later?) In the primary school at the Colegio Americano, the grim, intimidating atmosphere created by the professors and directors led me to carry out a singular provocation: I asked my parents to let me take private classes in Russian. I never got beyond: this is the roof, below is the floor, this is my house. Like all seditious impulses of youth, my penchant for the language of the feared communists was short-lived. But I did learn the Cyrillic alphabet. Years later, in the adolescent years I am describing, I wrote a diary that, while not clandestine, was impenetrable. The texts, almost always dedicated to Helena Rojo, were in Castilian but transcribed in Cyrillic. I still have the notebooks in some trunk or other.

Incidentally, when I was sixteen years old, my father and I lived out what might be considered a roguish variation of Turgenev's *First Love*. He began a love affair with a young South American actress, whom, in the fashion of a nineteenth-century Russian novel, I will call A_____ . When my father broke up with her, she came to see me, no doubt hoping to recover his love. But he had gone on a long trip, and as the reader of that Russian short story may already have guessed, A_____ and I began an affair of our own. Later, when my father returned, he called her on a whim, and all of a sudden they started up their relationship again. I stepped aside without protest, in silence. When he once again grew bored with A_____ , my father used me as a pretext to get rid of her. He told her that he had to stop seeing her because she had created a problem with her constant visits to the house. He told her that I had fallen in love with her and was suffering more and more every time that I saw her.

It is possible that he based his fiction on a true fact: he saw me one afternoon looking out of my window and sighing. Only I was sighing of love for another, as we all know, and as A____ knew as well, for in the brief prelude to our love affair we had been confidants. My father's deception was painfully transparent. And we never saw our A_____ again.

Anyhow, I was proud of what I considered my own parcel of passionate complications. I would share them with any friend with secret boastfulness. But my intuition told me that while they might represent a kind of personal treasure, and while they seemed strictly spiritual to me, they were worldly subjects that I should not share with Buñuel, because they would not be to his liking.

All the same, I am strangely certain that these early, precocious experiences gave me the necessary inner fabric that made my friendship with Luis possible.

Soon, I dropped out of high school to work in the cinema: as head of production, assistant, various jobs of little importance that, along with my home movies and the schooling I had received, became my stairway to the desired world of the cinema.

I want to emphasize that I never found an intrinsic value in entering a career, be it for freshness or verve that can accompany such an early start. Nonetheless, I was directing my first full-length feature based on my own screenplay at nineteen.

During those years working as a young professional, I talked with Luis less about movies and more about life. Surely Luis guessed that one of those situations that I preferred not to talk to him about was worrying me, and he said to me:

"Be Careful, Saint Thomas Aquinas. Just because it's more difficult doesn't mean that it's more meritorious...

Walter Achugar, Manuel Michel, unidentified person, Arturo Ripstein, Alberto Isaac, Luis Alcoriza, Luis Buñuel, Frantishek, Gabriel García Márquez, Antonio Matouk, and Gloria Marín. (Acapulco, 1966)

Julio Alejandro

Julio Alejandro de Castro was a very lovable old Madrilenian: short, compact and robust, of strong features, as if his face had been cut out of tough wood by an inexpert chiseler. A venerable homosexual, quite sentimental, a bit whiny, generous when it came to affection and friendship. Fastidious in manner, sometimes theatrical, though his voice would break in such outbursts of his rough-edged personality.

When I began to perform my experiments in the cinema, I used his house, that of a true antiquarian, as a set, and he appeared as an actor in two or three scenes. He sometimes came up with the most exquisite commentaries: "These films of yours," he said once, "remind me of Sibelius, his Tone Poems."

Some years later, in my first full-length film, the autobiography *Crónica íntima* (*Intimate Chronicle*), he played the role of my grandfather: a sallow and desolate effigy, almost a ghost.

Julio was best known for collaborating with Buñuel on five scripts, including *Nazarín*, *Viridiana*, and *Tristana*, and he worked on the set designs of other of his movies. He was more or less Luis's age, and I had the opportunity to witness that he was one of the very few that addressed him with the informal *tú*.

Not infrequently I heard him saying, "Well, Luis, if you don't like it, you can go to hell…"

Someone, I don't remember who, told me that during the

filming of *El ángel exterminador* (*The Exterminating Angel*) Luis needed a rug to resolve a last-minute problem with a set: a large drawing room that two or three characters would have to cross. Julio disappeared to get the article the director required. After a while, he arrived on the set with a tiny Chinese rug of forty by fifty centimeters. He held it up to show it to Luis, who grunted:

"What is this piece of shit?"
"It's the rug."
"It doesn't work. It looks like a handkerchief."
"But Luis, it's from the Ming Dynasty."
"It's a piece of shit."
"Luis, go fuck yourself," the delicate Julio finally shouted, offended, affronted, and disconsolate.

Julio Alejandro embraced by Claudio Isaac at an award ceremony, ca. 1977

A Test

In one of his wicked moments, Luis invented a story about Julio in which he had gone to the hospital to take a *prueba de esputo* [sputum test] and that a very severe, emotionless doctor had given him the results, telling him, "Señor Alejandro, the test results were in fact positive: *es puto* [you're a faggot]."

His Friend

Although she always maintained a sentimental fixation with my father, very soon after their separation my mother went to live with a man quite a bit younger than she. This never failed to provoke protests and criticisms from those who surrounded her, including her closest relatives. As one might guess, Buñuel did not approve of my mother's new relationship. But in time he was won over by the man who, like the gentleman he was, greeted him with a smile and a slight bow of his head. Relations moved from mere tolerance to a level of civility and cordiality: he ended up visiting my mother's house, where I found him dining there two or three times. I remember above all one afternoon in which we were having fun striking theatrical, exaggerated, and comical poses

Luis Buñuel and Lucero Isaac, ca. 1963

for a camera that was not working; all the pictures turned out blurry. Later, knowing that he had us all entertained, he did a few demonstrations of hypnotism. Although the proceedings were also theatrical, Luis became completely sober—no joking here, as it was a serious matter.

Referring in indirect fashion to the situation my mother found herself in, living as she was between reprimands and social condemnation, Luis touched on the theme of slanderous gossip.

"It's contagious," he said. "With these ingredients, conversations can become interminable, and the details and anecdotes proliferate. On the other hand, if someone says: what a great marriage so-and-so have, the response is a monosyllable and then nothing else. Yawns. The conversation falls flat."

When he took his leave that day, Luis seemed worried about his friend Lucero, my mother. While Jeanne went for the car, he approached her and spoke to her in a murmur that could be heard close by: "Lucerito," he said to her, "you can handle everything, can't you?"

Tell Your Mother Hello for Me

"Mexicans don't like the Spaniards' way of talking; they say it's too coarse. And the figure of the mother: oh, how carefully she has to be treated. As they always prefer diminutives, *madre* sounds very rough to them; one should say *madrecita*. If I say tell your mother (*madre*) hello for me, they will answer me: Up yours, son of a bitch."

Luis smokes his cigarette and blows out smoke. He concludes, laughing:

"Then one should say: *Por favorcito*, tell your *madrecita* hello for me."

Kid

The rendezvous is at the restaurant of Mr. Hevia, an old friend and patron of my father. The specialty of the house is kid. I don't remember the occasion for the special dinner. I see Luis arrive in a wool suit that he wears only once in a blue moon. He is also wearing a bowtie, which makes him look like a schoolboy at first communion, a good little boy.

The other guests choose between two conservative options: leg or kidneys. In the purest spirit of surrealist provocation, Luis orders head of kid and later explains: "I love brains. But above all, I love the clicking sound when my teeth bite into the kid's teeth…"

Gabriel García Márquez, Alberto Isaac, Florentino Havia (the owner of the restaurant), Carlos Savage, and Luis Buñuel, ca. 1969

A Portrait

Spring 1973. Peals of laughter ringing in the air. A Luis anecdote, again in the restaurant that serves kid. Someone, I think it is Emilio García Riera, points to a mannerist oil painting saturated with pastel colors and, jocularly declares: "It's the portrait of a friend of my grandparents, a very frivolous woman, a real whore..."

Luis turns toward the painting and frowns, faking surprise: "Hey, but that's a portrait of my mother!"

Titles

It's probably summer. For once we're on the terrace, in the shadow of a fig tree. For some reason I make a comment about those Japanese ink drawings of which the signature, also considered a work of art, is as important as the rest of the composition.

"Beginning with surrealism," Luis says, relating the theme to his memories, "it became clear how much value a title could have. Sometimes half the value of the work. Why? If, for example, a conventional romance novel is called *My Cousin, the Little Whore*, the title changes the entire content. Or, on the other hand, if a work full of sex scenes is called *The Little Lambs of the Pilgrim*..."

Luis, ca. 1969

Frankly

At a society dinner, the type the Buñuels did not usually frequent, a pretentious sculptor told Luis that his five- and six-year-old sons already recited poems by García Lorca.

"Tell me, maestro," the woman asked him, "about the times that you shared with Federico García Lorca, of your literary soirées..."

"Whenever Federico got ready to read his poems," answered Luis, somewhat annoyed, "I would say that I was tired and was going to bed..."

"He would tell me: You're a fool, and I would reply that he was a wannabe and his poetry was kitschy [cursi]."

It was clear that the woman wanted to cut the conversation short, and she had started to take her leave when Buñuel had the last word:

"He would show me a poem and I would tell him, frankly: Federico, this is a piece of shit..."

Blush

Luis had an anecdote from his Jesuit school that he greatly enjoyed because of its silliness and told it quite often: One day it was his turn to give the Latin lesson. The teacher, evidently wearing a cassock and a grave expression, said to him:

"Now let's see, young Buñuel…Go to the front of the class… Decline the Latin verb *puto*…

Luis is in front of the class and the wait becomes tense. He knows the answer but doesn't say anything. Most of his classmates also know the answer; they have repeated it a thousand times, and they have invented humorous variations on it. This makes the ticking of the passing moments even more unbearable. No doubt the students are excited by the malicious expectation of what they know is coming.

"What's wrong, Buñuel?" asks the teacher.

Finally, young Buñuel, his locks falling over his very serious face, decides to respond:

"*Ego puto*" [I am a faggot]

And despite the choir of murmurs and nervous laughter, he continues with the variations: *Tu putare, ille putarem, nostrum putatis*, or something like that, until the classroom explodes in hilarity and disorder.

It was always disarming and moving to see the little Aragonese boy — medieval and innocent — alive in Luis; showing his purity, showing how so many years later that same
spirit of childish mischievousness that he shared with his
classmates made him blush whenever he told the story.

Commonplace

In one of his last formal addresses, in 1982, after six years of absolutely reckless spending, President López Portillo made an unpardonable gesture of sentimentalism: with tears in his eyes, he asked forgiveness of the oppressed of the nation. Buñuel was furious. I saw him the next day, and he was still fuming.

"So he gets emotional and weeps in front of the assembly, fine. He should recognize his misdeeds. But to shed tears just as he mentions the oppressed is abominable. If I'd been there, I would have taken out a revolver and shot him in the head. That's what I call *risum paillase*."

Buñuel had told me — and I'm surprised that this is not recorded elsewhere — that for the hypocrisy of sentimentalism, for pathetic pronouncements, so detestable to them, Dalí and he had invented a word, a mixture of Latin and French, that entered into the surrealist code: *risum paillase*. The clown who laughs for the world but cries inside. The phony profundity of that abject commonplace.

Correcting and Inventing

I believe it was when he had finished *Le Fantôme de la liberté* (*The Phantom of Liberty*) that he returned with the news that he had filmed with the help of a video monitor from whose image he could give stage directions without getting up from his chair.

"I have the cameraman exasperated: move forward, a little more to the left, a little bit more to the left...now down...like that all day long..."

And he concludes with a comment of exaggerated but genuine modesty:

"And, of course, it's easier to correct than to invent: he's the ingenious guy, the creative one."

Tango

Although Luis usually kept up with politics and current events, he sometimes revealed endearing anachronisms. This takes me to a small incident in the sixties that my father told me about: one night in the Buñuels' house, where the Alcorizas, the Buñuels, and my parents had gotten together, Luis put on a 78 rpm record on his antiquated gramophone. It was a tango. When he started to dance with my mother, everyone else roared with laughter after Alcoriza commented:

"It's now confirmed that Luis hasn't danced since they took down the dance hall from the second floor of 'La Coupole'—and I'm talking about 1930..."

Lucero Isaac and Luis Buñuel

The Second Castle

"When he works as an assistant director of some of my films, my son Juan Luis is incredibly diligent and efficient. Perhaps too much so. If we need to film in a chateau, he locates five or six. He wants me to see them—all of them—and so we set off immediately. We see one that's not bad. When we see the second, I say: this one is perfect. But I have four more for you to see, Juan Luis insists. I don't want to see any more, I tell him. And the reason, which I don't share with him, is that the second chateau has a terrific bar right across the street..."

Authors

Although Buñuel was averse to change in so many things, set in his ways and personal creeds, he was irritated by fools. Experiencing mental rigidity in his friends or colleagues would never fail to disturb or infuriate him.

"Talking with Rodolfo Usigli about the possible screenplay for *Ensayo de un crímen (Rehearsal for a Crime)*," he told me one day, "I became convinced that as a general rule authors are morons and one should avoid them because they're hopeless. Usigli insisted that the conversation between the protagonist, Archibaldo de la Cruz, and his friend be filmed all the way from the Monument to the Revolution to the Zócalo of Mexico City, just as one follows the characters' stroll in the novel. We have to, it has a symbolic meaning, he argued. But that's thirty blocks, Rodolfo, I explained. And he insisted, it has a symbolic meaning. What a pain, they all go on like that…"

The Director and His Actors

With his deafness came a curious clumsiness. For example: his habit of always turning his shoulders along with his head or his way of bending forward as he walked, as if he were going uphill, but in a horizontal plane.

I never saw him direct, but often, when he was telling an anecdote about filming, he would act out what he was telling. Something makes me think that, unwittingly, he transmitted this clumsy, wooden manner: suddenly, when I'm looking at sequences in his films, it seems possible to interpret the peculiar dynamic of the scenes, slightly ceremonious and not very graceful, as a phenomenon of mimesis — unconscious, of course — of the actors with the director.

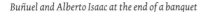

Buñuel and Alberto Isaac at the end of a banquet

With the President

Considering it a minimal tribute to the adopted country of the filmmaker, and knowing that Luis would not agree to a public act of homage, my father arranged for President Miguel de la Madrid to go to the Buñuels' house for dinner. It seems that the only other guests besides the president were the Dominican priest Julián Pablo Fernández and my father. Jeanne and Luis served a frugal dinner. It couldn't have been any other way. I can perfectly imagine Luis saying a word of warning: No caviar, Jeanne, because they are going to believe that we want something from him. While they drank cocktails, Jeanne showed them her new toy: a device that makes hard-boiled eggs in the form of a cube.

"Would you like to see a cubed egg, Mr. President?" she asked, smiling.

They also drank champagne and, later, cognac. At about eleven o'clock that night, Jeanne approached my father with pursed lips and questioning eyes—a gesture she didn't try to conceal—and said to him in that soft voice that was never quite a whisper although it was meant to be:

"When is this guy going to leave?"

"This guy" was none other than the President of the Republic, who must have overheard Jeanne's comment.

For various disagreements with the regime, my father would renounce his position in the Institute of Cinema a few weeks later.

At home, Buñuel with Alberto Isaac, President Miguel de la Madrid, and Father Julián Pablo

Luis died a couple of months after that dinner. I understand that that unusual social event, which was more impersonal than others they usually had, was the last one my father had with him.

Followers

Perhaps the films of John Ford, Fritz Lang, or Kenji Mizoguchi could be reproduced shot by shot in a new history in which nobody would discern where the shots come from. Such is the classical transparency of their styles. But it's not like that with the convulsive nature of Buñuel's images. The characteristic elements of his world are, as in the case of Fellini or Bergman, impossible to emulate. He who tries to do it reveals himself immediately as a plagiarist.

The significant appearance of insects, dwarves, or priests, the sacrilegious humor or the irruption of unmeaning in the middle of a meticulously coherent scene: all of this discloses the guiding hand of Buñuel. There are even those who have imitated Buñuel's use of music in his last films, forgetting that the man couldn't hear when he made them.

He was not flattered by having followers, whether discreet tributaries or shameless imitators.

"*Jodorowsky*, or *Fuck*owsky, to me, is FuckingRipMeOffSky," he would say, not angrily but with disdain.

Sons

Rafael and Juan Luis, the Buñuels' sons, used to tell how they had to hide snacks in their socks when they left for school because their father had them on a strict diet and didn't let them eat very much. They always left for school hungry.

That is an anecdote from the brothers' childhood. But even when they were adults, when they were both over forty, equally surprising things kept happening to them when

Luis, Juan Luis, and Rafael Buñuel, Mont Whisson (October, 1941)

they arrived at their parents' home to see their mother and the satrap of the house.

"If you go out, don't come back later than ten o'clock," he would tell them.

Sometimes they weren't given copies of the house key, and Luis, worried and annoyed in equal measure, would lie awake for hours, waiting for them. If they got home after the indicated time, Luis would receive them with an expression of genuine anguish: "Where have you been?"

I can visualize the scene: illuminated by the light of the main door, two corpulent men, both almost six feet tall, before the slightly emaciated figure of their father in a robe.

On learning, for example, that they had simply been drinking coffee with the Pecanins sisters, women of their age who owned an art gallery, Luis would mutter:

"Those *girls* are a bit degenerate, dangerous....Just look at what time it is."

Logic

During the rainy season he preferred that they not use Jeanne's royal blue Volkswagen:

"In the rain, no. Because it gets wet, it rusts."

Jeanne wasn't convinced by this logic; in fact, it embarrassed her a little to tell others of Luis's reasoning, but she ended up following his arguments.

Luis, ca. 1969

Books

On Jeanne's instructions, I inherited some of Luis's books. Some by Carpentier, and old editions of Arthur Schnitzler translated by Moreno Villa, a friend of the family. We almost never coincided in our literary interests. I idolized Borges in those early years of my life, but Luis truly despised him. I suspect that the aversion stemmed from a sort of unconscious identification on various points on which they coincided. He didn't like to see himself reflected in the elderly blind man who was only a year older than he.

For example, I think about the horror that both experienced when faced with the idea of copulation, which, like mirrors, Borges tells us, multiplies man. The very word copulation, an uncomfortable expression for both, implicitly carries an embarrassing sensation for these two strangely chaste men.

Now, completely by chance, I remember two lines that would have fascinated Buñuel if he were not aware that they were penned by Borges:

In the exact center of the web
there is another prisoner, God, the spider.

(*En el centro puntual de la maraña*
hay otro prisionero, Dios, la araña.)

Condemnable, Condemnable

The surrealists were rabid pursuers of their own brother-hoods, and as a result they almost always ended up going their own ways. They fought among themselves because of their fundamentalist fervor for purity and for obscure and labyrinthine disagreements; they were irreconcilable, in a word, because of their intransigence. Sometimes on top of their general dogmatism they would add that of Marxism, which so many of them would follow, in an imperceptible decline, an uncritical somnolence in the times of Stalin-ism.

Buñuel felt that he had kept a safe distance from the core of the surrealist movement. But it seems to me that certain parts of his personality were affected by the contagious fa-naticism and inflexibility that characterized this group of iconoclasts. That is, he was sometimes as rigid as the blind-ed subversives and the out-of-control dissenters around him who, though formidable characters, were led by their sectarian zeal and virulence against one system to support another one that was as just as terrible.

Buñuel was always indignant in the face of intolerance, yet he had to fight his own tendency to be intolerant, a tendency he was at times able to temper thanks to his intelligence and his sense of justice.

He once affirmed publicly, "I have always refused conces-sions and defended the principles that I stand by." He also said, "What I have always insisted on is not to compromise in matters that I consider morally essential."

Even allowing for the subjectivity of any interpretation, if one puts critical pressure on the worst of his films such claims simply fall apart.

In his nights of insomnia I imagine he judged himself by these tyrannical rules and found that he didn't pass the test.

I believe he was tremendously severe with himself almost all of the time and often with other people. One case in particular comes to mind from the late 1970s. Luis was furious with Arturo Ripstein, who had just made a commissioned film, in his words "shamelessly, for monetary reasons."

"The surrealist morality does not allow for such a thing even if one is dying of hunger," declared Luis with the severity of a judge. "Condemnable, condemnable …"

I also disagreed with Ripstein's actions at that time — he was, one might say, my mentor, and what he did disappointed me greatly — but Luis Buñuel's reaction reached the point of fury, and suspiciously so. Nothing is more irritating than spotting one's own faults in others. There is the possibility of compassion, putting oneself in the other's shoes, and taking pity on that person. But Buñuel opted for a total rejection and closed himself off. I wonder to what extent the supposed concession of Ripstein reminded him of the painful times in which he had had to have his arm twisted and to maneuver any which way he could in order to save his dignity before the world and himself.

Like Nietzsche's dragon slayer who becomes a dragon himself, it is a mystery of the human soul how the rival of tyranny sometimes metamorphoses into a tyrant.

León

Although at home everything was as orderly and precise as the mechanism of a watch, some things seemed to come out of a world turned upside down. Jeanne liked to show off the tricks of her dog, León, Tristana's successor, also a small white terrier with black patches. She would put the dog by her side on the main armchair by the bar. She would keep asking me to shake her shoulders or act as if I were going to strangle her. León did not react at all during this pantomime.

"On the other hand, look at this," said Jeanne, when hitting my chest repeatedly with her open hand.

Surprisingly, when his mistress attacked her guest, the dog growled and jumped at her with bared teeth.

"Can you understand that? Can you understand?" asked Jeanne, smiling.

I should add that León was not given his name as a mockery of the king of the African jungle. Rather, he had the name of a person, such as Tolstoy.

León

Antecedents

This book has existed for many years in germinal form: note-books from the time in which the events took place, sheets of paper on which I had written down anecdotes and reflections. And, above all, images that return time and again from the depths of my remembrances of things past. They are, for me, affectionate memories.

On various occasions I tried to begin writing it, but I was discouraged by the sense of being false, arrogant, a usurper. Many told me that the centenary of his birth was the ideal date for publication. Understanding my repudiation of that kind of opportunism, my friend Pascal Martí, a drastic reductionist, proposed the following: write the book and put it away in a drawer; in that way it's written even if you don't publish it.

For a while I considered this proposition very seriously. Later, I dropped the whole project and tried to forget about it. But the memories — and the emotion that accompanies them — kept returning. A fragmented memoir, a rough sketch, I told myself. A book *with* Buñuel rather than a book *about* Buñuel.

A Pair of Pugilists

In the innocent vanity of a man getting on in years, Buñuel liked to brag about his still-steely abdomen with muscles as hard as bricks. He would lift his jacket and say:

"Punch. Punch with your fist. Hard. Harder."

He smiled, satisfied with the surprised reaction of those who felt as if they were hitting a wall.

In the transition from my boyhood to early adolescence, I passed through a phase in which I went crazy about sports in general, and boxing in particular. This phase was short-lived, however, and I'm still not sure if this brevity was a blessing or a misfortune; I have to admit that I've always wished for a slightly more rugged complexion.

When Luis found out about my new pastime, he gave me the pear-shaped punching bag with which he trained daily at home. After that, he began to exercise in a club. In the showers of that sports club he slipped, fell, and broke a rib. All of that so that I would give up my week-long career as a pugilist, the shortest in history.

Gazpacho

Luis enjoyed eating well, and he loved to share good food with his friends. But not so much at home, where the rules of monastic custom held sway. I ate with him there very few times.

The first time, in the company of my parents, I was eleven years old. Until then I had been an only child, a kid that had been spoiled by the cook of the house, who, like a pampering nanny, only served me what I liked.

In the Buñuels' home I was in for something new. To begin with, they served gazpacho, prepared by the host himself in an exceptional gesture. This cold appetizer contained some of the ingredients that I hated most on the face of the earth: cilantro, onions, and raw tomatoes. I had to overcome my supreme revulsion, compose myself, and eat it all so as to not be dismissed by that adult society. Luis didn't pay any attention to me, but I am sure that he would have never forgotten a bowl of his gazpacho left untouched by the *Isaacs' kid*. It wasn't that he was a proud cook, but any pretext would have been a good one for him to put me in my place. That bowl of uneaten gazpacho would have followed me to the end of my days.

Informal Address

Luis didn't like being treated like a demigod, and it often seemed as if he wanted to step down from a pedestal. Indeed, there was a circle of adoration surrounding him, a solemn retinue that would ingratiate themselves to him and never dare to contradict him. These were the people who addressed him with the formal *usted* and called him don Luis. The classification may be too broad, but it holds good. Submissive and condescending, they were too impressed by Luis to treat him as a man of flesh and blood.

It came naturally to me to use the informal *tú* with him since my parents had always spoken to him that way. In their case, more than a mere modality, it was a sign of a relaxed and easy-going relationship, and although they clearly respected him, they didn't stand on ceremony. For this reason, and because Luis became something like a second grandfather to me, I was able to approach him with total familiarity, from greeting him with a kiss on the cheek and hugging him every time I saw him to confronting him on simple but fundamental subjects.

"Why are the actors in such-and-such a film so stiff? Why is the ending of that other film so clumsy? Isn't that scene change too abrupt?"

It was not arrogance or irreverence, as some of the older people present interpreted it; I wasn't so blind or thoughtless. But neither would I wish to attribute my comments of disagreement to the merit of intellectual rebellion. I insist that they were simply the advantage of that inheritance in the way of addressing him.

Point of View

One time I witnessed how Alcoriza was arrogantly explaining a convoluted theory about a cinema without artifice. "But the cinema is artifice by definition," I tried to tell him, and he continued, satisfied with himself.

"I don't use background music. In a movie the music has to be justified by the presence of a radio or record player. If not, where does it come from? It is an artificial device…"

But I was even more perplexed by another one of his theories:

"The sensibility of a cinematographer doesn't matter to me, only his heftiness…"

"And why is that?" I asked, alarmed.

"Because he has to be able to support the weight of the camera. No tripods, that language is out of style, it's dead…"

Although he would not have commented on the matter, the truth is that Buñuel thought those long, single-shot sequences filmed with a hand-held camera in Alcoriza's recent movies were abominable.

"That isn't even justified as *pov*," declared Buñuel.

"What the hell is *pov*?"

"It's 'point of view,' an abbreviation used in screenplays... Well, not even as a point of view of somebody is it acceptable...

"It's not acceptable..."

After a reflective pause, Buñuel smiled and grimaced, adding:

"It's an epileptic camera. Dreadful...Luis uses it to not feel over the hill, to prove that he's a young guy, no other reason..."

The Alcorizas

Always, ever since I was a child, I have thought of Luis Alcoriza as an extreme case of fatuity. Janet, his wife, was brilliant and cultivated without flaunting it. But she rendered him this service: she organized ideas for screenplays, edited texts, worked in various capacities so that he could succeed as a director.

Luis Alcoriza was not very discreet in his pursuit of the actresses that he courted, seduced, and dropped or used in the film he was working on at any given moment. In spite of this, he maintained an enduring complicity with Janet. She didn't play the role of victim. She adored him, but she wasn't submissive in the way that Jeanne Rucar was with Luis Buñuel.

Also exiled in Mexico, the Alcorizas had been actors. Luis had played the role of Christ in the theater and also later in a film titled, I believe, *Jesus of Nazareth*, in which he acted with notable dignity despite the biblical atmosphere that surrounded him. Later he established himself in the recurring roles of indignant boyfriend, the city dandy in westerns, the suitor who is replaced by the leading man in a cowboy hat, Pedro Infante, Jorge Negrete, or any number of popular actors of the time. And Janet, under the name of Raquel Rojas, dressed as a flamboyant flamenco dancer and with a Viennese accent, performed for villains of the Axis nations in unrealistic films of international espionage.

He came from a family of traveling Spanish actors; she came from a fairly prominent Austrian family: her father, the musician Hugo Riesenfeld, was a friend of Schönberg, Zemlinky, and other members of the *entartete Musik*, the moniker with which the Third Reich stigmatized the work of avant-garde composers, whom the regime considered, literally, degenerate. That rich family history of Janet's was reflected in her best conversational moments, in her critical opinions. Both were hard-liners, somewhat intransigent and dogmatic in their leftist opinions, as was typical of the times.

When their careers intertwined, Buñuel was like a mentor for Alcoriza, given that he had greater experience and prestige. The Alcorizas were a little better off financially than the Buñuels when they arrived in Mexico, and they were both generous and supportive of Luis and Jeanne. They recommended Luis for various jobs; as my mother tells me, they gave Jeanne furniture for the house. (Months before dying, Janet proved her prodigious generosity once again by making me a gift of her records, including rare recordings of pre-Baroque music and a stupendous collection of Richard Strauss.)

Alberto Isaac and Luis Alcoriza

I return to Luis Alcoriza. His every word and gesture were those of a macho show-off. Subtleties tended to annoy him; to him they were for faggots. Sometimes he gave the impression of not being willing to capture from the external world more than the sound of his own voice. He wore tight, short-sleeved shirts to better display his biceps and pectorals. I have already mentioned his preference in trousers. He liked sports cars, the most extravagant ones. Sometimes he would appear at gatherings still wearing his pilot gloves and with aerodynamic chrome goggles to give the finishing touches to the picture.

I always respected Luis Alcoriza because he was one of my parents' friends I knew throughout my childhood, but I never liked him as a filmmaker or as a human being. Nonetheless, I realize as I write this, I felt, and still feel, affection for him.

From my father I learned that at a festival at Cannes, profiting from the fact that Buñuel was not there but was asleep in his bed across the ocean, Alcoriza made statements taking credit for some of the stylistic trademarks that the world had come to call Buñuelesque, though it was obvious that he was the imitator and, at that moment, a common stand-in. I reflect on those statements today and recognize that Alcoriza was too vain to be a bad person: he didn't have time to worry about others. The wrong he did stemmed from his vanity. My father, who was present at that press conference, was furious about the way Alcoriza belittled his friend, but he preferred not to say anything to Buñuel. Perhaps Luis never found out, or only suspected, but he really didn't want to know. I think that in his final years he came to understand the true nature of Alcoriza but never stopped caring for him.

In countless things, Alcoriza was obviously opposed to Buñuel, but his relationship was a healthy counterpoint: a constant friendly rivalry, many arguments in the form of shouting matches, but, in the end a harmonious rapport. Always much festivity.

I have written at length about the Alcorizas because they were a key couple in Buñuel's life in Mexico. The two Luises worked together on more than ten screenplays, and three or four with Janet as well.

Before and, more particularly, after Luis Buñuel's death there has been a sordid dispute about his person: Who was his best friend, the closest? For whom did he predict the most triumphs? Whom did he consider his true successor? Faced with such base behavior on the part of directors, actors, producers, writers, artists, and film critics, it seems urgent to me to declare that, as far as I can see, there is no room for doubt: followed by Julio Alejandro de Castro, the closest to Buñuel in his own country (and probably in his entire life) were the Alcorizas. By a long shot. They and, later, Father Julián.

Father Julián

Julián has been a polemical priest, without doubt because of his intellectual restiveness. Besides reconstructing temples or forming workshops for street children or other social work, he has dedicated himself to painting and the cinema.

He also promoted a splendid film club and headed a cultural center at the university. The first time I saw him in that center, before entering his office, I happened to overhear how he had absolved a parishioner with an unorthodox penitence: instead of giving him twenty Our Fathers to say, he suggested that he listen to a classical music station for half an hour every day for one week. This detail, which I found out without his knowledge, won me over immediately.

In addition, Julián was friends with Juan Rulfo, Octavio Paz, José Luis Cuevas, as well as figures from bohemia and from the boisterous world of the cinema and theater. This alone left waves of suspicion and sanctimoniousness in its wake. But what really stirred people up was his close relationship with Luis Buñuel. More than the gossipy conjectures and the anticlerical resentment, he was bothered by the jealousy some felt because of his closeness with Buñuel, an undeniable fact that, as I have said before, his detractors tried—and keep trying—to discredit.

Julián also used the formal address of *usted* and called him "don Luis"; nevertheless, he was not part of that submissive, flattering group that would so often besiege Buñuel. Perhaps he was the exception to that curious rule. Nearing the end of

Observed by Julián Pablo Fernández: Jeanne Rucar, lipstick in one hand and mirror in the other

Luis's life, they saw each other almost daily, and I am sure that more often than not it was Luis who called Julián. He would pick up the phone and call him, something he didn't do for anyone else in the world.

Janet

Innocently, Jeanne revealed an indiscretion concerning Janet Alcoriza:

"She took advantage of her thick dark glasses to doze off during the *sobremesas*. If anyone asks her opinion about something, she has a French phrase that works in any situation, in any situation she repeats it: *C'est incroyable...*"

Luis and Janet Alcoriza soon after their arrival in Mexico

To Speak Clearly but Not Very Loudly

Cinema itself was not a favorite theme. I don't know if the reason was discretion, modesty, or simple indifference. It was his expressive medium, but undoubtedly the cinema was not his entire life, the range of his interests went way beyond it.

I find that the friends of the filmmakers, the critics, tended to speak to him of technical aspects, the movies, and the directors then in fashion. Of course, all of that represents a slice of life. But Buñuel was interested in everything about the world, all its mysteries great and small. At that time I was also excited about cinematographic novelties, the latest facts, trivia. But soon I understood that Luis's most profound concerns lay elsewhere, and the last thing I wanted to do was to importune him. I defended my ideas, I expounded them, I supported myself with them, and even, as I have mentioned, I questioned him. I also dared to approach him in a humorous tone, but always making sure through the signs I was learning that he was in a good mood. I never dared to antagonize him. In fact, seeing him bothered or wearied mortified me.

In other words, it was not the man of transcendent talent that I feared but rather the unreflective, easily annoyed, obsessive man that he became, an irascible man plagued by aches and pains, a man with one good ear into which one had to speak clearly but not too loudly, *diction, not volume.*

When I visited his house, the weight of the enormous difference in our ages would sometimes crash down on me, and I would feel truly lost.

Cloister

Without a doubt, Luis had a latent fierceness, which at times could make his house feel like a cruel cloister, an ogre's lair.

Luis, ca. 1969

What They Left Us

Any student of surrealism will tell you that this movement combined characteristics that had already appeared in the art of writers and artists ranging from Bosch to Kafka, from Quevedo to Goya or Lautréamont, from Rabelais to Erik Satie or Julio Ruelas. It distilled a preexistent spirit and assigned it features, targets. At the same time, surrealism represents a kind of new and innovative platform, a point of departure that unfetters the creators of the future, granting them the freedom to explore dreams, the absurd, the automatism of the unconsciousness, playful arbitrariness, vindictive venom, or pure poetry. To properly evaluate what they left us, it would help to establish some limits. It may be one of my deranged notions, but I have always thought it more important to consider the surrealist movement in a historical way—as a phenomenon—than according to purely esthetic criteria.

The Two Halves

There is no place where the asymmetry of Luis Buñuel's face is more evident than in the study of the two halves of his face made from the frontal portrait that Man Ray did of him around 1928.

On one half of the face the nose is more rounded, the thicker lip rises a little in a semicircle, and the drooping eyelid gives his gaze an air of bovine nobility.

In contrast, the other half features a more pointed nose, the mouth twists downward with disenchantment, and the eyelid is decidedly more open, leaving the iris more separated from the white of the eye, which is very awake, or better yet: that of an insomniac. An eye that distils temerity.

Duplication of half-faces of Luis Buñuel from a photo by Man Ray

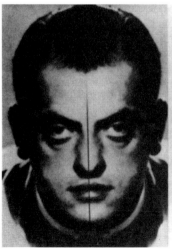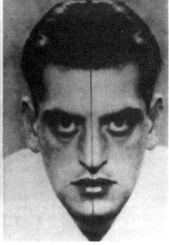

Just as the alchemists had their guide of magical anatomy, in which they identified astrological signs with parts of the human body — Aries, the head; Tauro, the neck; Cancer, the chest — I am tempted to locate in that contorted and powerful face of Buñuel his different attributes. Or a list of his

Man Ray's portrait of Luis, ca. 1928

contradictions; his dichotomy. On one side, his timidity, loathing of drunks, erudition regarding religious themes, jealousy and possessiveness, insistence on domestic order. On the other, his fondness for masks, love of drinking, philosophy without God, detestation of bourgeois values, the scruples of an iconoclast and a subversive.

I find myself frequently trying to reconcile the reticent man that I knew, whose home was his castle, with the exhibitionist, the man of the streets, who, in the twenties, paraded around Paris dressed up as a nun. I am convinced that his proclivity for scandal stemmed from a conviction of ideological order and for that reason survived over the years.

But, of course, I end up explaining the coexistence of so many contrasting traits as something perfectly natural through the flashes that I was able to witness in each of his many sides: they were, all of them, Luis Buñuel.

Close-Ups

When he began the filming of *Subida al cielo* (*Ascent to Heaven*), Luis had the idea of playing a joke on his actors, a pair of novices.

"I called Lilia Prado," as Luis tells the story, "and also...that guy who is in the film with her, a florist, I don't remember his name..."

He is referring to Esteban Mayo, a young, first-time actor who besides acting also had one of those typical flower and gift shops and who is famous today for his telephone Tarot-card reading service. Once Lilia and Esteban Mayo were in front of him, he looked at them very solemnly, with the terrifying seriousness he adopted when playing jokes of this kind.

"I have called you," he says, "to tell you that the union has given me permission to charge you for each close-up that we do of you. So, since I am an honest man, I am telling you now so that you do the math and decide how many close-ups you are going to want..."

The actors retire to deliberate. When they return to speak with the director, they have figures in mind.

"Lilia, very sweet and timid," Luis says, "asked me for only twelve close-ups. In contrast, the florist, well off and a bit vain, asked me for more than thirty... "

"Later, I found it difficult to make them understand that it was all a joke. I repented having done it. They were both very upset. Actors are from another world."

Jeanne and Luis, recently married

Interview

One cold day, Luis and I are in the bar. The doorbell rings. Jeanne appears, and addresses her husband from the entrance hall:

"Luis, some reporters have come to see you...they would like to interview you."

Almost without looking at her, he responds, dryly:

"I'm not interested..."

She insists, appealing on behalf of the visitors; she surely sympathizes with them:

"But they've come from Madrid."

Luis, in the same tone:

"Tell them no..."

And Jeanne, in a last attempt:

"They say they're from a workers' newspaper..."

Without a pause, he answers:

"Then tell them I'm a fascist..."

Before Eating

"Figuerrroa?...Figuerrroa?..." With her French "R," Jeanne called out this name, projecting it down the hallway toward the kitchen. We are in the drawing room by the entrance, just about to go to the table.

"Figuerrroa," the woman repeats, shouting even louder. Luis pays no attention; he has a distant look on his face. The rest of us don't know Jeanne's intentions, and we begin to wonder if something is wrong. After a pause, she begins to think out loud:

"Figuerrroa,...Figuerrroa...Gabriel Figuerrroa...

Gabriel, Gabriela...Ah, yes, Gabriela!"

She begins to shout again so that she can be heard in the kitchen:

"Gabriela?..."

From the end of the hallway we hear a faint voice:

"Sí, señora?"

"Gabriela," Jeanne shouts again, "is the meal ready?"

"Sí, señora."

In this house the past and the present are intermingled, as are the memories. Dialogues become silent and thoughts are expressed out loud.

Two Actresses, One Role

This I know from my father: Luis told him that he was disillusioned after his unpleasant meeting with Maria Schneider, who was going to interpret the role of Conchita in *Cet obscur objet du désir* (*That Obscure Object of Desire*); he wanted to abandon the project and go home. The first thing that occurred to him was to make an absurd, over-the-top proposal to Silberman, the producer: that the main character be portrayed by two actresses, indistinctly.

"Two actresses in the same role, you're crazy," was what Buñuel imagined the producer would tell him, sending him off on the first flight to Mexico. As is well known, the story did not turn out like that, and Buñuel's return home came much later: the outlandish idea for the film worked as an innovation; it was applauded and transcended its accidental origin, becoming a perennial source of interpretations that, in the end, enrich the subject.

A Great Beard

The anecdotes abound of Buñuel's actors who, in the middle of filming, were disconcerted by his hermeticism, who didn't know if they were doing things right or not, always suspecting that there existed a master plan of which they were unaware, who suspected that they were being used in a game being played on a higher plane.

In *Simón del desierto* (*Simon of the Desert*), the hermit, bearded and in rags, withdrawn from the world, is played by Claudio Brook. He tells of how weeks of filming passed without Buñuel's making a single comment. He found out that at night Buñuel and his crew went over the filmed material of the previous days, and yet he still didn't hear a single word from the director about his acting. One day, having reached the point of desperation, he approached Luis and confronted him, asking:

"Maestro Buñuel, how is my work going?"

To which Luis responded, mispronouncing the last name of his protagonist:

"Hey, Brus, well the beard, the beard is great, the beard is really great, Brus..."

Sculptor

I continue to believe that Buñuel was a more philosopher than a filmmaker. In general his movies are filmed rather clumsily, the mise-en-scène is usually stiff. Given the industrial contexts, his Mexican films are a little worse than the Spanish ones, the French films a little better but not much. In fact, I believe that a richly textured image or outstanding technical know-how are both essential to Buñuel's true discourse, which is subterranean. In effect, the *esteticismos*, as he called a feared and hated formal brilliance, would have lessened his impact.

One day I told Luis how shoddy and unimaginative the final shot of *Los olvidados* (*The Young and the Damned*) seemed to me. He answered sincerely and calmly:

"Kid, you're right. The only thing on which I pride myself is the rhythm of my films: there isn't any wasted time in them. As for the rest, perhaps I should have been a sculptor..."

Carlos Savage, Luis Buñuel, and Alberto Isaac

Sculptor, Philosopher, or Filmmaker

The cultural and educational environments are infested with unreflective, solemn veneration; people worry about not breaking worn-out golden rules and fall into the most despicable insincerity. Nobody admits that Joyce can sometimes be excessive, Foucault tedious, that Beethoven at times overdoes it, that a genius can become heavy-handed, or that Buñuel always offers something curious but that many times he is faulty and his films are untenable. Just consider how awful some of his films are: *Gran Casino, El gran calavera (The Great Madcap), Carne y Demonio (The Devil and the Flesh), Abismos de passion (Wuthering Heights),* or *El río y la muerte (The River and Death),* among others. Like so many other admirable figures, Buñuel has been deified, and this worries me. When a distorted image is created, lacking human error, in the long run, in the eyes of new generations, the virtues can also lose their validity, corrupted as they are by falseness.

I have always taken issue with the position that unconditionally approves everything Buñuel made, creating a monument to genius without fissures. In this modern-day brand of orthodoxy, people call such mediocre films such as *El bruto (The Brute)* or *La joven (The Young One)* masterpieces, basing their arguments on some spark of talent, some casual symbolism, or a transcendental subtext of some film or other.

Yet I unreservedly admit my admiration, as I have in other moments, for a singular phenomenon of implacable nature: imagine someone, a neophyte of the cinema, turning on a television set, flipping randomly through the channels, and by chance coming across a scene from a Buñuel film that he has never seen before. It doesn't take more than a few moments to perceive the gravitation of a visual singularity that is both perturbing and unforgettable. The viewer would see that Buñuel's cinema is, in its own percussive way, poetic: it is a world with its own rules and dramatic climate, with its own particular rhythm, or heartbeat, which makes it unmistakably different from the other orbs in the cinematic universe. Sculptor, philosopher, or filmmaker, there is and there will only ever be one Luis Buñuel.

Luis, ca. 1974

In the Bookstore

"In Paris, Jeanne had a friend, a certain Miss Beach, who lived on Rue de L'Odeon...Sylvia was her name. She owned a bookstore, 'Shakespeare and...something.' It was just a very small room full of portraits of writers and, of course, books too. One afternoon, when I went to pick up Jeanne, I met a man there in a dark overcoat, with a patch over one eye, sitting in a corner. I disliked him immediately for the way he looked at my fiancée's legs. (This was right before our wedding.) Well, this guy who looked at Jeanne's legs so insistently with his good eye — a deep blue eye that seemed enormous through his thick glasses — was James Joyce."

Sylvia and Jeanne in the bookstore

Joyce

When I was sixteen or seventeen, I was obsessed with Joyce. And with him, his life of hardships and intransigencies. I was enthralled by his notion of *epiphanies*, or the most evanescent moments, and the idea of the artist as a collector of epiphanies. I wanted to read Joyce into everything, throw him into any conversation, relate him with any theme that came up. At that time, I persuaded Buñuel to tell me the above little vignette, then unpublished. What affected me most when I listened to him were the precise names of people, the street, and the description of "Shakespeare and Company," all of which was fresh in my mind from what I had recently read in books, references to a lost age of the golden mist of the beginning of my century.

Joyce

Hotel Room

Among my papers, I find some beginnings of letters. For example: "February, 1975. Dear Luis, The years separate us but we are closer than appearances would suggest. I hope you have a good trip. Your accomplice, C. P.S.: I will be imagining you, there on your balcony, with a view of the tombs."

Surely the postscript now requires an explanation: I was still a child, traveling with my parents, when I stayed in L'Aiglon, the hotel that Luis Buñuel recommended in Paris. "It is not ostentatious," he said, "and it is close to everything."

We took neighboring rooms, one of them Luis's usual room, in the rear part of the fifth floor. Or maybe it was the seventh. What surprised me most about that sand-colored building from the early 1900s was the interior decoration in the worst taste of the sixties: flying buttresses like bunches of grapes, furniture upholstered in explosive colors, and an imitation leopard rug that was impossible to ignore. Ostentatious rooms, no, but not discrete either. It would have been difficult to visualize Luis there were it not for the contrast the view offered: the metal *art nouveau* balconies overlooked the Montparnasse cemetery. The lugubriously beautiful landscape is worthy of a painting of the Romantic painter Caspar David Friedrich. And, for the same reason, common tourists stay away from the place, which always seems deserted. The inevitable conclusion is that this is the true reason why Luis preferred this hotel.

My Notebooks

Some of the meetings with Luis are recorded in notebooks from those years. Sometimes, I concisely register a visit: "July, 1981. I went to see Buñuel to listen to his opinions after his last reading of my screenplay. He doesn't seem to like it, and in general I don't think he understands what I'm trying to do. He gave me, as always, good pieces of advice, and he treated me with affection. When he said goodbye, he said with a smile: "I read your screenplay again though I haven't bothered to read screenplays, even of friends, for the last fifteen years. Only because I love you a lot..."

At other times the entries are even more hurried and almost telegraphic: "August. Meeting with L.B., we hardly talked and we agreed to meet next Thursday."

It occurred to me that in order to establish a counterpoint, or in order to clarify a little better who I was then, that beardless interlocutor of Luis Buñuel, I could include some of the many texts of my profuse notebooks from the seventies and the beginning of the eighties. Choosing the passages almost at random, it is with a mix of antipathy, compassion, affection, and laughter that I look upon this young man who was sententious, dogmatic, and pedantic, plagued by premonitions, superstitions, preoccupations, and guilt regarding purity and goodness, honesty and transcendence, even in one of its least noble guises: personal fame. There is as much levity as solemnity, shyness and insecurity right beside petulance:

MAY 1972
"The passivity that waiting imposes bothers me. And the air of speculation that it generates. Speculation can be creative

but it can also immobilize us, just like superstition: it has that power. Life is a long wait, divided into short periods of waiting..."

JUNE 1972
"Optimism is a form of evasion."

FEBRUARY 1973
"One of the possible political attitudes is to contribute to the worsening of society in order to create a crisis that will unleash changes."

Drawing in crayon, ca. 1989

"It is easier to invent great conflicts than to sit down and admit the simple and unattractive truth: it is not destiny, or fatality, or extreme sensibility, or sharp intelligence [*inteligencia*]; it is merely adolescence [*adolescencia*]. (And the rhyming is involuntary.)"

DECEMBER 1974
"Piety is contemptible; it implies contempt."

JANUARY 3, 1975
"The accumulated weight against our liberty is such that only in excess do we find equilibrium."

JANUARY 10, 1975
"Perhaps pain is where the true intensity of life is found. Joy can never be as intense. This arbitrary judgment describes an emotional state, not my capacity for reason. Long live subjectivity."

FEBRUARY 1975
"The memory of ridicule is the most powerful of all. It is when the past is more present than ever."

MARCH 10, 1975
"I'm writing this note just before going out. The time I have spent on it is taking away from some meeting, maybe the one I had been truly hoping for."

MARCH 18, 1975
"I recognize that look: you are formulating your next sentence while I still haven't finished talking. You don't listen to me."

"Faking insolence or indignation for reasons that really don't mean anything to us: a way to test the nature of others, to disconcert them, to make them unwittingly reveal their hypocrisies and false pronouncements."

OCTOBER 1976

"Forgiveness helps the person who gives it grow not only before those that receive the apology (which is of less importance), but also before oneself. Asking and giving forgiveness is related to self-esteem."

DECEMBER 19, 1976

"He gives essential importance to small matters in order to hide himself from the underlying question."

DECEMBER 20, 1976

"The art dealer: You look my drawings over systematically with an eye to the future. You don't appreciate the possible values of my work, the work in itself; you only measure its possible commercial consequences and sale possibilities. It is depressing to meet people like you."

DECEMBER 29, 1976

"A curious relationship between the Manual of Epictetus and the passage of Albertine's death in Marcel Proust's *The Fugitive*. Both, curiously, speak of stoicism. From opposite shores."

JANUARY 1977

"Simple cinematographic montage unites two essences. Dissolving can make the effect of conjunction of essences obvious and cause it to be read as easy symbology. If we carefully observe, we realize that the whole world is related. In other words, we don't have to emphasize the matter. It is about being conscious of it. This state of consciousness in itself will come through in the work, it will be present without our insisting on it."

FEBRUARY 1977
"A trip. Only by living with a person does one come to love that person. The day arrives in which affection is discovered: it's already there, it moved in."

MARCH 1979
"Screenplays lack their own light. I commented on this with Luis Buñuel the other day. Writing screenplays is a not a very gratifying labor because they cannot capture the vivacity of the images, they only suggests them, and apart from the possible merit of the dramatic structure or the quality of the dialogue, they lack literary value. As long as they are not made into films (and this can take many years), they are neither one thing nor the other. Neither literature nor cinema."

I Saw Him Dancing

Like a good *baturro*, or a typical Aragonese, Buñuel mixed up some words, above all those of foreign origin. He would call the cineaste and antique dealer Raúl Kamffer "hamster." He would confuse "hamster" with "monster," "cassette player" [*casetera*] with "coffee maker" [*cafetera*]. All because he was distracted, because he didn't think it important.

Before a meal in my mother's house to which Julián had been invited, Luis thought of a joke that he wanted to play on him. Some comments had been made to him (that were true this time) about the worldly life of Julián, who stayed out in bars and discotheques until late. Luis got various accomplices together and said to them:

"You all surround us when he comes to say hello to me. I am going to lay in to him about his late-night carousing; I'm going to pretend that I am scandalized because I saw him dancing in a ...a discotheque. You all remain serious, no friendly faces, no smiles...Completely serious..."

When Julián arrives, Buñuel begins to speak to him in a scolding tone, starting with a complaint about how late he has arrived for the meal. Then he follows his previously drawn-up plan, but he makes the others laugh before he can finish because he muddled up his speech:

"Julián, last night I saw you dancing in...in a cinema-theque..."

"In the discotheque..." someone said, cuing him.

Julián Pablo, Buñuel, and Sara Elías Calles

"That's it, in the discotheque..." Luis said, correcting himself, but he was already laughing along with everybody else.
He gave Julián a warm hug, shaking with laughter.

Authority

During the filming of *Nazarín*, before shooting an outdoor scene, Buñuel concentrated on reviewing the costumes of a couple of dozen extras.

Meanwhile, Gabriel Figueroa, the prestigious cinematographer, tried to anticipate all the instructions of the director and ordered that the rails be placed for a complex movement of the camera, a long traveling shot.

When Buñuel finally appeared in front of Figueroa, who fancied himself a director, the cinematographer invited him to mount the dolly and watch through the camera to see what the visual evolution would be of the shot that hadn't been asked for.

Dissimulating his displeasure behind an apparent docility, Buñuel acceded to do the trajectory over the rails. On finishing, he turned to Figueroa and said quite cordially:

"Well, Gaby, this take is gorgeous...

But tell me...What movie is it for?"

As I've said before, I never had the chance to see him direct on location, but I can imagine how he would have exercised his silent authority, without insults and without tussle. Also, I'm sure what his reaction would be to subordination of any kind, although it might appear, as in this case, under a mask of extreme efficiency.

With Paz

It's two-thirty in the afternoon. I return home in the suf-
focating high school bus. It's a scorching summer. I go to
the kitchen and drink some cold water. I hear voices in the
dining room and take a peek: my parents have invited the
Buñuels and Octavio Paz and his wife, Marie José, who have
just come back from India. They've already sat down to eat. I
slide into my chair at the end of the table. Suddenly, halfway
through the meal, Luis sniffs an empty wine glass.

"You see, Jeanne," he says with the glass in his hand, "this
glass has been washed well. It doesn't smell of soap."

Jeanne sniffs her glass, with her nose in it.

Alberto and Lucero Isaac, Jeanne Rucar, Marie José and Octavio Paz, Luis Buñuel.
Drawing, 2001

"But there's no need to exaggerate," snapped Luis. "Why are you sticking your nose in it?"

Luis imitates Jeanne, with his nose into his own glass. He sniffs loudly.

"Why are you doing that?" Jeanne complains.

"You're the one doing it like that..."

"But you...you do it so much worse..."

Now Jeanne imitates Luis with exaggerated gestures. Although the scene is hilarious, at first the others stay on the sidelines and assume the role of silent spectators. Later, when they realize that they are not witnessing a real domestic dispute, laughter arises that envelops everyone, including Jeanne and Luis. Jeanne makes a comment about my hair, which has darkened and is no longer lank. She looks at me with warmth.

After coffee I go to my room to do my homework. With Luis I haven't exchanged words at all, even to say goodbye. In contrast, Octavio Paz knocks on my door before leaving and asks permission to enter. The room is very small but has a skylight in the middle that bathes it in sunlight. He runs his eyes over my bookcase. He draws close to it and looks at a few titles.

"They're all yours?" he asks with a gentle smile. When I say that they are, he adds, "And you read them all, don't you?"

It was the only time I saw Paz when I was a child. I like to think, however, that this scene of friendliness and interest for me prefigures in some way the abbreviated but beautiful friendship I would develop with Octavio when we worked on a film together twelve years later. Like that with Buñuel a little later, a privileged relationship of my childhood.

Voices

I was in the finishing stages of my film *El día que murió Pedro Infante (The Day Pedro Infante Died)*. I needed two voices, a man and a woman, to assemble a sequence: a young woman a bit frustrated with her aspirations, now an office worker, dreams about her parents. In the scenes, somewhat nightmarish, the latter two characters are merely silhouettes projected against a wall.

I asked Jeanne and Luis if they would loan me their voices for the shadowed parents. The dialogue goes as follows:

Luis: "...Well, the piano teacher says the girl has talent..."

Jeanne (almost interrupting him): "But it wouldn't be good for her to get her hopes up high about something that isn't going to be of any use to her in the future..."

I never suspected what this event could have as a background. Many years later, after Luis's death, when Jeanne was going to publish her *Memorias de una mujer sin piano (Memoirs of a Woman without a Piano)*, I learned the reason for the title: it seems that soon after getting married, Luis exchanged her piano for a case of champagne. In an act of jealousy and egoism he had cut short his wife's musical career. The fact upset me, it gave me goose bumps: when I made the recording of their voices for my movie, I had unwittingly given them the wrong roles, I had inverted them. But the words were so cruelly close to the true story.

Drawing, 1994

A Retreat

To write a cinematic adaptation of Rafael F. Muñoz's novel about the Mexican Revolution, *Se llevaron al cañón para Bachimba* (*They Took the Canon to Bachimba*) in a tranquil setting, Julián invited me to spend a week at Tultenango, a Dominican convent that, it was said, was haunted by the ghost of a crazy nun. She never appeared to me. On the other hand, I had the chance of living with the extraordinary figure of

Alberto Isaac and Luis Buñuel, 1963

Father Jaime Gurza, an admirer of Bruckner and Kierkegaard. An elderly man, Gurza sat at the head of the table at mealtimes and twisted the ear of a dog to make her howl. Even then the dog, Chiquita, did not leave his side and followed him the entire afternoon.

In theory, this retreat was similar to what Luis customarily took with his collaborators when they were writing a script. But we were never able to escape our urban rhythm, and we worked nonstop, finishing very quickly. Within a few days we had finished the first version of the screenplay and returned to Mexico City. Julián gave it to Luis. After reading it, Luis said that we had mitigated the violence too much, the direct brutality of the original. The protagonist, Alvarito, was an adolescent from a well-to-do family who joined up to fight in the armed resistance against the government. Buñuel did not like our portrayal of him.

"That Alvarito...is a bit bland. A bit dull."

"He's like an intellectual from the city...But don't say that to Julián. My opinion isn't important..."

Buñuel valued discretion, and it is likely that he sincerely regretted having emitted that evaluation, especially since he knew that we were hopeful about the project. Understanding the natural objections of Luis to our screenplay, Julián and I amused ourselves imitating Luis passing down his devastating verdicts.

Jeanne's Book

Memorias de una mujer sin piano (Memoir of a Woman without a Piano) is a book that Marisol Martín del Campo constructed delicately from the memories of Jeanne Rucar, then a widow. Originally it was going to be titled *La cocinera de Buñuel (Buñuel's Cook)*, but Jeanne thought that was perhaps too violent. She told me this herself one day, as if she were proud of a secret bit of mischief. For those who are familiar with the way Jeanne usually expresses herself, it is obvious that her words, her way of expressing herself, have been polished, converted into literature, but not as a personal affirmation on the part of her ghostwriter. The transformation has been nobly achieved, by virtue of the transparency of the discourse. The innocent soul of Jeanne surfaces intact in these pages.

I read the book in one sitting on a morning of a May 10. Because it was Mother's Day, that seemed to me a fitting, amusing pretext to call Jeanne and congratulate her. I imagine her, practically blind, coming from the kitchen to the nook under the staircase where the telephone was kept. A concave space that produced an echo; when he was alive, a torture for the nearly deaf Luis.

"Congratulations, Juana, I've read your book..." I told her, calling her as usual by the Castilian version of her name.

"Congratulations?" she answered. "For the book or for Mother's Day? Because don't forget you're my son...I cured you of colds..."

I said that I was congratulating her for both things. But above all for the book. An unthinkable achievement if Luis had still been alive. She said she was very pleased, and declared:

"In the book I don't tell a single lie, everything is told just as it happened..."

Inevitably, my thoughts went back to Luis's memoirs, which, in part because of the complacency of his collaborator Jean-Claude Carriére, in part because it was an intellectual biography rather than a rigorous recounting of events, has an element of artificiality, of that retouching that is absent from Jeanne's book. And also because Buñuel shows the face with which, then an old man, he wanted us to remember him. It's not that that face is touched up with makeup, but that it lacks some of his most endearing features as an individual. Please understand that I am not trying to diminish the formidable quality of Luis's book as a document, its brilliant passages, its sometimes explosive declaration of principles, his vision of the world. But it doesn't read as a well-rounded work of literature; it seems uneven in form, though it's impossible for me to get out of my mind the beauty of his words when he says that "dreams exist only for the memory that caresses them."

In contrast, Jeanne's memoirs possess a natural and organic way of breathing, a unique voice of an almost infantile immediacy, of absolute, unbounded honesty. In the same way as she spoke to me on the phone.

Rustic

Pierre Drieu Rochelle reflects: "Atheism has achieved nothing: throw Saint Peter out the door and Freud comes in through the window. Throw Freud out, Aeschylus and Sophocles remain."

Inspired, André Breton conceives a current that frees daydreams, rage, madness. Pessoa would write: "The sentiment with which they desire paganism is Christian." In a similar vein, Breton never manages to strip himself, paradoxically, of Descartes as well as Voltaire; rationalism and enlightenment resound in him, even in the darkest impulse, and that lineage from which he never knew how to free himself filters and diminishes, dilutes the impression he pursues, its efficacy. For better or for worse, at that moment French tradition was the center of Western culture, and the French surrealists drag it along with them in their search for novelty, in their attempt to begin from zero, to liberate themselves. And something of the scaffolding of that rational tradition remains in the finished work that wishes to be purely oneiric, following only the dictates of the unconscious.

To my mind, Buñuel realizes the ideals of surrealism — subversion, shock, and shaking up the spectator's conscience — much better than his contemporaries do because, among other reasons, he comes from a rustic and backward province. Ravel's *Bolero*, with its manifestly sophisticated orchestration, loses all kinship with the roll of the Calanda drums, however interesting the percussive effect may be. And Buñuel is a son of that barbarous Calanda and its drums. For that reason, even with his philosophical ideas and poetic vision, his art is telluric. In this respect I agree with the recent interpretations of Buñuel by Carlos Fuentes and Penelope Gilliatt.

I would add that another important, very important aspect, is Buñuel's individuality: a sensibility that for love of simplicity presents things bluntly. I am tempted to say that too much adornment also has been a disadvantage, in the long run, in the French heritage: from creamy and well-seasoned food, to Corneille, to art-nouveau, one finds delicious embellishment, but mere embellishment. In point of fact, an unpropitious quality to achieve the causticity desired by the movement. But I should backtrack a little: an austere discourse, without circumlocutions, like that of Buñuel, seems *crude* to us as much as it may be intellectually premeditated and elaborated. And crudeness is not only a sharp blow; it can also be interpreted as freshness, vivacity. The result, in short, would be a more lively surrealism, its beauty as blunt as that of an unpolished stone: a brutal beauty.

Discrepancy

As is well known, Buñuel hated to film kisses. On the other hand, be it fetishism or not, he liked shots of legs, separated from the rest of the body, as autonomous parts, and, more particularly, feet. Later, Gabriel Figueroa declared that Buñuel always wanted to shoot actors from head to toe, that he had no understanding of the "American shot" (a shot that frames the body from head to mid-calf). As in his biased comments on his collaboration with "Indio" Fernández, Figueroa never gave credit to directors and tried to suggest a partnership in which he was the aesthetic guide. I witnessed such outbursts of self-affirmation several times. I should make something clear: "Indio" was not an intellectual or an artist who graduated from an academy; while he followed his instinct in using a hieratic and overdramatized cinematographic language, he also developed a notably personal, fluid, natural, and unique discourse. One can see it in his films that were shot by Alex Phillips or Jack Draper, where Figueroa's absence does not become a demerit, for the man was, in fact, gifted with a great plastic sensibility. And yes, Buñuel could certainly be awkward, but he knew what he was doing and what he wanted. Luis himself used to say how, to shock Figueroa, he would change the angle of the camera that Figueroa had just proposed: instead of an impeccable shot of clouds, a municipal trash dump. And in fact this discrepancy with Figueroa (which the latter emphatically denies in news reports or interviews) was useful to Buñuel to support his thesis about the efficiency of the visual aspect of films, considering only that which possesses narrative or dramatic value of use.

Standing: Sigfrido García, Alberto Isaac, Emilio García Riera. Seated: Luis Alcoriza, Carlos Savage, Luis Buñuel, and José Luis González de León

Don't Kneel

"Luis, Did you see Kurosawa's *Yojimbo*?"

"Maybe. I get confused. Which one is it again?"

"The same as always, it's about samurais, a solitary hero."

"O.K."

"I found a piece of dialogue in the film I'm sure you will like."

"Tell me."

"Toshiro Mifune says it, with his stentorian voice, walking vigorously back and forth in front of a crowd..."

"What does he say?"

"Don't kneel before me because I could kill you all: I detest pathetic people..."

Luis looks and the horizon and smiles broadly, visualizing the scene with obvious pleasure.

"I thought you would like it."

"A practical guy...Cut their throats...I like that."

Milton and His Daughters

Another story that I once told Luis, guessing which strings would pull on his sympathy, is that of John Milton and his daughters. The poet, who I suppose was having a foreboding of his blindness, taught his daughters the phonetic rules of Latin but not the significance of the words. That way, later, when he was completely blind, he could have the perverse pleasure of listening to Petronius or Catalus or other authors of obscene texts from the chaste mouths of his daughters.

"Is that all true?" asked Luis.

"The basis, yes, what follows is speculation..."

"One imagines them sitting together in front of the fire," said Luis, relishing the scene, "everything apparently so serene..."

Etymologies

Besides his academic knowledge of Latin and his efficient use of an unadorned Castilian Spanish, Luis loved to invent etymological roots to dupe ingenuous listeners. He would cite the most improbable origin for words in his usual grave, doctoral tone of voice.

I remember him, once again in Mr. Hevia's restaurant, with a group of people at his table listening to his lengthy speech about the properties of a bottle of Hungarian wine that he was holding.

"Don Luis, you aren't wearning a tie," Carlos Savage says to him in the presence of Mr. Hevia. He puts his on tie on him.

"*Egri Bikaver.* That means 'go with God'" — and he elaborated: "egri-*vaya*; bi-*con* and kaver, of course, *Dios.* Go-with-God."

To his performance he also liked to add pedantic gestures and intonations, like a true erudite on the subject.

"Do you all know the origin of the word *sacerdote* (priest)?" he asked the group in his deadpan manner. "As is well known, *sa* is a Sanskrit prefix of uncertain significance, and *cerdote*, a disgusting pig (*cerdo*) of enormous proportions..."

The Man without Company

Buñuel declared once that in his version of *Robinson Crusoe* he wanted to concentrate on the theme of the lack of love or friendship, the loneliness and anguish of a man without company.

I have often thought of the solitary Buñuel in his last years or months as a Robinson, enclosed in his house with its thick, high walls, or, better, imagining the reduced zone of his neighborhood as if it were an island; beyond, nothingness. This line of thought takes me, whether I like it or not, to something else that the suicide Drieu la Rochelle wrote: "Robinson Crusoe has always seemed to me to be the symbol of humanity par excellence. A man alone, completely lost, who builds a house. And he does so because he imagines that someone is watching him and that what he has done will become known." This mixture of humility and transcendence was Luis.

One More Drink

In the seventies, a group of directors who belonged to an intermediate generation, including Felipe Cazals, Miguel Littín, and Jorge Fons, threw a dinner party for Luis. It was a barbecue and was charming precisely for its simplicity. At the meal there was an atmosphere of true joviality. People expressed their appreciation without being ceremonious. As had happened only a few times before, Luis was touched, visibly moved.

I took him home that night. On the way he was contented and silent. When I stopped at the entrance, he looked at me with a sparkle of warm complicity and invited me to enter.

"Only for a little while," he said, "because it's almost time for bed..." It was about seven o'clock. We went into the bar.

"Just one more," he said with a smile. While he poured gin in his cocktail shaker, he sent me to get something, olives perhaps, from the refrigerator a few steps away. I was looking in one of the compartments when I heard a hard, sharp sound behind me.

When I turned around, I saw Luis lying on the granite floor. A few seconds passed, and the nearly eighty-year-old man didn't move. I became alarmed. I knelt down and lifted him up by his shoulders until he came to. I helped him sit up. When he recovered, he looked embarrassed and surprised.

"This hasn't happened to me since I was your age, kid. This is awful! And I thought I knew how to drink..."

It was true. I understood that the drinks had affected him mainly because of the excitement of the get-together, because of the profound emotion.

His Support

In his last years, Luis Buñuel confided primarily, as I mentioned earlier, in Father Julián Pablo. I don't know what they talked about, and I haven't wanted to ask; since the matter is effectively one of confessional secrets, I consider it off limits.

What I can easily imagine, however, are their matches of wit. "Blessed are those who imitate me, for theirs will be all of my defects," Julián liked to repeat. One can also deduce that their dialogues were both philosophical and theological: they both shared a wealth of knowledge, which ranged from Saint Thomas of Aquinas and Ramon Llull to the Marquis de Sade. Curiously, Sade's *Dialogue between a Priest and a Dying Man* was one of their favorite texts even before they met.

I certainly don't mean to suggest, even remotely, that Luis had a conversion experience. That would be as improbable as seeing Julián turn into a heretic. From the position that Luis adopted at the conclusion of his life I like, as a kind of corollary, these words that he once expressed to the film critic Penelope Gilliatt: "I am not Christian, but I am not an atheist either. I am tired of hearing that old saying that I invented by accident: I am an atheist thanks to God. It's spent. Dead leaves. It is from the sense of guilt that we should escape, not from God."

The Lowest Expression

I had just finished editing my first feature-length picture and felt full of energy again after going through a period of tenacious doubts, when I went to visit Luis, this time in the afternoon. His attitude and his words took me as much by surprise as if the floor had crumbled under my feet.

"I'm fed up with the cinema," he began, as soon as we sat down. "It runs over people, it violates. It's the lowest expression that exists because it doesn't call upon, it doesn't need to call upon, the intellect,… everything happens so vertiginously and without asking permission. If it's even an art form, it's very inferior."

"But its potential…" I tried to argue. He interrupted me immediately:

"Its potential was left behind, buried. The reality is this…"

Idealist and imbued with a sense and literary vision of the cinema, I advocated the idea that it was the legitimate right of the filmmaker always to make demands on the spectator, to produce films that require rereadings.

"Impossible," he said. "The cinema is never going to be anything but an industry."

"What you are saying goes against the interests of this industry."

"All of this is crap…"

I didn't find a counterargument to his judgments or any way at all to contradict him. He dragged me along with his clouded spirit of that afternoon.

Alchemist

I have said that with respect to ideas, Luis could be more than severe, almost rigid. Just as he had unfathomable scruples, he also had candid attachments. These instances of unreflectivity, I'm afraid, were due not to age but to character. Certain subjects and key words would unleash in Luis a sometimes absurdly prejudiced fury.

For example, the word *estética* ("aesthetic") he could not swallow, but even less, as I have mentioned, *esteticismos* (aestheticims). I try to interpret it as follows: beauty is beauty

Luis Buñuel joking around with Carlos Savage

when it turns out to be functional, when it is contextualized in terms of the plot. If not, it belongs to something like the realm of the beautiful, the superfluous aesthetic, *los esteticismos*.

The word *metafísica* ("metaphysics") would also set him off. To explain this, we could consider his early encounters with Marxism and related currents. But we could also speculate about his quintessential coordinates: if we appraise the weight and value that Buñuel, in his films, gives to certain motifs, the mystery that he concedes in equal measure to objects, places, animals, and people, we understand his repudiation of claims that he was a symbolist filmmaker.

Neither symbolist nor metaphysical. Accordingly, he genuinely possessed the hermetic sense that everything obeys the same law: *unum in multa diversa moda*, Buñuel would recite to us in Latin in order to later translate it for us. With this in mind, I judge that he proceeds to relate it to the ideal of the first alchemists: spiritualize matter, materialize the spirit.

From a prejudiced Buñuel we pass to the hidden philosopher.

Winter

Luis did not often open the metal door himself to receive a visitor. It was a sunny midday but bitterly cold. After ringing the bell I waited for a shorter time than usual. He appeared in a wool shirt with a contented, gleaming look in his eyes. I kissed him on the check, as was my custom, but we embraced for longer than usual. The welcoming smile soon changed into a grave expression. On the way to the bar, he explained to me that he was alone: his wife had taken the dog out for a walk, and Gabriela, the cook, was at the market, she had forgotten something and had gone back for it. He told me all of this in detail as if to justify his being home alone. I

Portrait painted on wood relief, 1987

noticed that he was anxious, but I couldn't tell why. Altering the ritual steps of the preparation of drinks, he announced what would be the central subject of our conversation. Without prefacing his comments, he launched into his discourse, saying that when he was very young he had read a *Manual for the Filmmaker*, written by a Russian.

"It's stamped on my memory," he said, while he poured gin into the chrome-plated cocktail shaker, "what the author of the book, I forget his name, listed as the indispensable attributes of a film director: total lucidity and impeccable physical condition. After that come technical questions, but those first two..."

There was a pause and he cast me a quick glance, adding:

"As you know, kid, I don't meet those requirements, the ones the book that gave me so many helpful hints, from which I learned..."

In what followed, I tried to emphasize the fact that technical advances could resolve the question of physical condition and that he was clearly as lucid as can be. I tried, that is, to give him support and encouragement. But it was impossible. Maybe I myself believed, deep down, in the arguments of that manual. I was in the presence of a man who had already taken a crucial decision, which he was now sharing with me. Undoubtedly he was announcing to me his retirement from filmmaking.

He was almost eighty, and his painful stance, besides being dignified and clear-headed, also followed from an unshakable logic. What was worrisome was how that decision might affect the natural evolution of his state of mind: besides being deaf, he was almost blind in one eye, and immersed in a web of daily relations that he himself eroded with his authoritarianism, that he impaired with the shadow of his oppression. Because of medical prohibitions the last things that could give him pleasure were forbidden: trips to cold Europe, good meals, wine, and tobacco.

Soon, on top of all of this, he would also have aches and pains of which he would never complain openly. He mentioned them with the descriptive conciseness that must have been a remnant of his short scientific career, his study of insects: he listed the illnesses, he described them in detail in an attempt at arriving at some humoristic observation. But the human person was also disappearing, and for the same reasoning that he quit the profession, as well as his inextinguishable modesty, he also distanced himself from his friends, even his closest ones.

I return to that cold midday: the sound of the door closing reached us, and Jeanne arrived, greeting us from the doorway while León ran directly to his master's legs.

We had become completely immersed in the conversation, and only then did we realize that we both had tears in our eyes. To my surprise, as soon as his wife arrived, Luis tried to soften his face and attitude and even attempted to trivialize the situation with jokes. My visit might seem to have concluded on the familiar note of any other day at the Buñuels'. Now, however, I understand that during that day there was much ceremony, a liturgy of farewell.

Two Hallucinations

I know that though he tried his best to be stoic (it was his true nature), in private, Luis sometimes gave in to cranky and even catastrophic moods. Aside from Jeanne, his sons, and Julián, probably no one saw this side of Luis. Maybe, only maybe, his doctor.

In his final days, when Luis was very sick, he was plagued by hallucinations. Julián, distraught, told me about two of them in a moment not of indiscretion but of unburdening. I wrote them down in a notebook in April 1983.

One time, when he was lying down for his daily after-lunch siesta on the terrace of the second floor of his house, he saw a long stick with a yellow ribbon tied to the end of it; it was scraping against the bars of the balustrade making a disagreeable noise. Luis went down to the first floor to see what was happening but couldn't find any stick or anyone who might have been holding it.

On another occasion, Luis wakes up in the early morning and sees his room full of smoke. He shouts, "Jeanne, Jeanne, the house is on fire!"

Jeanne enters his room and the smoke has disappeared.

Price List

I don't omit capriciously. I forget. Although I search for se-
renity, my pained memory produces torturous turns. How
many times did I see Luis cry? How many times did I cry
along with him? Only a few times, but I no longer know
how many.

After writing the previous chapter about tears, I recalled
(I believe correctly) that the last time I saw Luis when he
was alive, he was fixated more than ever with the subject of
bombs — not as an aspect of terrorism but with explosions
in themselves. But beyond that not much else. I was sad
to realize that what he could remember accurately was no
more than a price list of the different products on sale in the
large department store on the avenue in front of his one-way
street. On how many solitary afternoons, I asked myself then
and I ask myself now, must Luis have wandered around the
inside of the department store, that maze of display cases
and aisles of shelves, meandering aimlessly?

Between the Walls

Jealous, misogynist, negative, Luis created a situation in his home that, as one might imagine, would eventually turn on him. Jeanne's condition as his slave, the way in which Luis never let Jeanne blossom, accentuated throughout the years. And with a slave one can't have a relationship of companionship or complicity. As a result, in his last years Luis couldn't share with her some of his most terrible moments. He also kept secret many of his spontaneous inspirations, ideas for screenplays, founding images for stories. He no longer had a wife with whom he might talk about intimate things, transcendent questions, urgent concerns. He couldn't do that with the woman who, for the last forty years, had slept in the room next door.

I imagine him so lonely, wandering through the hallways of that empty house, between the walls of stone, his feet freezing from the cold of the mosaic floor, his whole body growing chilled as well. Trapped in a web of his own making. Lost.

Eternal (July 29, 1983)

I suppose that it happens frequently with some long-lived mythical figures: having met him when he was already old, I grew up with the idea that he was eternal. Eternal, though perhaps he was the first person in whom I detected those stains on the hands that, not without a shade of the macabre, people call *flowers of the tomb*. Eternal with all those progressive aches and pains and his illnesses, which were becoming more frequent. Eternal his profound gaze. His death, when it came, left us shocked and overwhelmed with sorrow.

Alberto Isaac and Luis

To Luis Buñuel, on the Day of His Death

It seems to me that so many hours in the hospital weighed too heavily on you; too many bottles of serum, the medical instruments, the white uniforms, and the humiliating atmosphere of murmurs that surrounded your room, that surrounded your bed. All of that weighed on you and penetrated your lethargy. For this reason, this afternoon, while you napped, you dreamed that you were dying.

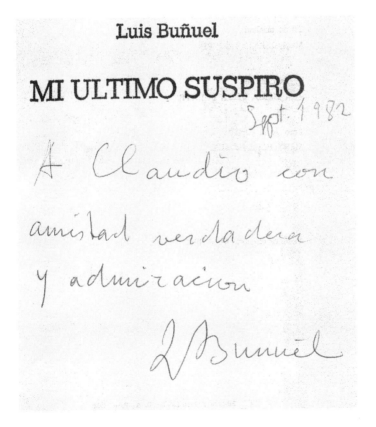

Luis Buñuel

MI ULTIMO SUSPIRO

Sept. 1982

A Claudio con
amistad verdadera
y admiracion

L Buñuel

Legacy

Of course, Buñuel's films left their mark on me as a spectator, but not as a budding filmmaker. It's clear that, in my case at least, the legacy of Luis Buñuel has little to do with that. He wasn't a mentor of cinema for me, but he was (with all the discrepancies that the reader is already aware of) a tutor for life. A tutor for life. His great lesson for me is simplicity, modesty, an indifference to material things, his ethical steadfastness and his fight to achieve congruence, his loyalty in friendships, his consciousness of the relative value of all things in life, of the paltry nature of fame, ambition, and presumption. He left his solidity, his rectitude, his unswerving dignity. And, above all, his posture of not taking himself too seriously, his resistance to ceremony, not only in others, which restrains one's own liberty, but also in his own thinking, as it constricts and asphyxiates.

What Did I Give Him?

"The sympathy that exists between two persons, between various persons, seems to put them on the path to solutions that they would not be able to reach alone." This idea of André Breton's used to console me when I thought about the ultimate meaning of my friendship with Luis. But not anymore. I have mentioned what Luis gave me, what he left me. But what could I have left him?

Although I was more melancholy than enthusiastic, I must have provided him, with my youth, a comforting breeze, a little contagion of vivacity, mental excitation, and also love. In particular, physical warmness: I kissed and hugged him often; as I have mentioned, he was like a second grandfather. But, in conclusion, what did I give him? Besides love, I'm not really sure. I don't know. Maybe that was enough.

December 28, 1990

I meet up with Jeanne, Juan Luis, and Rafael. A meal. The atmosphere is tense because of the rigorous exclusion of *his* name, *his* person, which is carefully avoided at every moment. Without mentioning him, today he is present as the *great absence*.

Luis and Jeanne, ca. 1969

April 3, 1993

In her book—an example of how ingenuousness can be more caustic than ingenuity—Jeanne Rucar, the faithful wife of her dead husband, comments, "In truth I am not alone, Luis continues to be present in my head and my heart. I always see him here, at home. I can't get over his absence..."

When I visit Jeanne, I don't even stop to consider the gravitation of that specter which, not exactly having gone *to the other side*, dictates the domestic order: obedience to schedules and customs. It is not the *phantom of liberty* but rather that of rigor. Or, perhaps, on another level, it is that of liberty achieved through rigor.

Jeanne and Claudio, ca. 1988

Disarrangements

Jeanne invited me to eat at the house. Juan Luis and Rafael were also expected; they had just come from abroad with their children, on a visit to their grandmother.

Altering the tradition, I rang the bell two minutes before twelve, the hour of aperitifs. I had already killed time looking at window displays on the avenue Félix Cuevas so that I would not arrive too early. With two minutes to go, I grew impatient and was tempted to disobey the old rules of the game. One could say that this unchained a whole series of ruptures and disarrangements from the quotidian, from the disorder in the arrival of the rest of the group at the table to the chaos of a broken-down oven, an uncooked chicken, burned rice.

When I rang, the sons were not yet there. Walking in the dark, Jeanne soon came and opened the door. We went to the terrace, not to the bar. Contrary to custom, we ran out of conversation very quickly. Normally, if we exhausted all the current topics, we would have on hand any number of anecdotes or reiterative references. This time the only fact of that kind was: "I've known you for thirty years, how incredible." She was holding my hands, her eyes fixed on mine though she couldn't see them. Afterwards, the laconic expression of sharp pain: "I don't lose my bearing. But it's terrible being blind."

To Stay

Sometimes I've been asked: What did Buñuel feel about Mexico? I don't know exactly. But it must have been for some reason that he stayed here; Juan Luis and Rafael spent their formative years here, only later — and here is an enigmatic story for another day — to return to their respective cities of birth, Paris and Los Angeles.

For some reason, when he had retired from filmmaking, Luis stayed in his house at 27 Cerrada Félix Cuevas, and died in Mexico. For some reason Jeanne, as a widow, didn't abandon that house with its unmistakably Mexican fig trees and ivy. For some reason she stayed here, even though it implied living alone.

She was suddenly beset by blindness, and in her resolution not to give in to decline she dedicated herself to knitting. At first she handed out scarves, shawls, and sweaters to family and friends as gifts. Later, she kept channeling so much of her endless energy into making so many other knitted garments that there was no one left to give them to. A Homeric Penelope, widowed, blind, and insatiable for life, who no longer waited for her husband but kept knitting. No doubt in winter, in the harshest cold of February, she would go out to the nearby streets and, with the help of the cook, would give away blankets, wool vests, and warm clothing to the anonymous indigents: the forgotten ones, *los olvidados*.

Dream

JANUARY 2001

Surely influenced by the days that I have been evoking the figure of Luis to write these pages, I dreamed about him.

I saw him in the garden of his house, in an area of shadows formed by the vegetation and speckled with spots of light. I was in my bathrobe, disheveled, just out of bed, when I saw

Drawing in pencil, 2001

myself beside him. He wore a white, short-sleeved shirt and sand-colored trousers. He looked at the house from top to bottom.

"I came to see why it hasn't sold," he told me. "It's not that I'm so interested in the fate of the house, but I suspect that it has something to do with these trees..."

He pointed to the fig tree. In my dream I was sure that I was dreaming. I could perceive Jeanne's presence inside the house: steps of high heels on the granite floor of the kitchen, a slight movement of the curtains.

"You returned for that?" I mumbled to myself.

"For that," he answered, leaving me not a little surprised: he had completely recovered his hearing and was showing it off.

"I can hear everything, everything," he said, standing there placidly.

He closed his eyes in deep concentration, holding up his hand not as if he were directing a film but as if he were conducting an orchestra. Suddenly a fig fell from the tree onto the grass. Then Luis opened his eyes and confirmed my suspicion:

"I heard that too. And you, how are you doing?"

I explain to him that I am finishing this book. He gives me a disconcerting frown that soon disappears: he definitely doesn't approve, but he closes his eyes again and smiles.

When he saw this picture taken by Lucero Isaac, ca. 1969, Luis commented, "We look like a disgusting bourgeois married couple."

Illustration Credits

Claudio Isaac created the drawings that appear in this book, with the exception of the cartoon on page 15, which is by Alberto Isaac.

The photographs are reproduced from originals in the personal archives of the Isaac family.

The material about Janet and Luis Alcoriza was made available to Mr. Héctor Delgado, to whom the author expresses deep gratitude.

"Photograph of Buñuel" © Man Ray Trust / Artists Rights Society (ARS)

About the Author

Claudio Isaac was born in Mexico City in 1957. Self-taught, he is a painter, filmmaker, and writer. He has previously published a novel, *Alma húmeda* (*Humid Soul*), and a collection of poems, *Otro enero* (*Another January*). "I've based this book," says Isaac, "on loose notes in a notebook from twenty to thirty years ago. The tone of the book is the result of a lengthy decantation, the final result of a friendship that left its mark on me and that I have been working through in my memory for a long time."

Swan Isle Press is a not-for-profit publisher
of poetry, fiction, and nonfiction.

For information on books of related interest or
for a catalog of new publications contact:

www.swanislepress.com

Midday with Buñuel
Designed by Jill Shimabukuro
Typeset in Dolly by Underware
Printed on 55# Glatfelter Natural